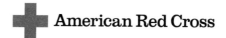
American Red Cross

head lifeguard

Important certification information

American Red Cross certificates may be issued upon successful completion of a training program, which uses this textbook as an integral part of the course. By itself, the text material does not constitute comprehensive Red Cross training. In order to issue ARC certificates, your instructor must be authorized by the American Red Cross, and must follow prescribed policies and procedures. Make certain that you have attended a course authorized by the Red Cross. Ask your instructor about receiving American Red Cross certification, or contact your local chapter for more information.

American Red Cross

head lifeguard

Mosby
Lifeline

St. Louis   Baltimore   Boston   Carlsbad   Chicago   Naples   New York   Philadelphia   Portland
London   Madrid   Mexico City   Singapore   Sydney   Tokyo   Toronto   Wiesbaden

Mosby Lifeline
Dedicated to Publishing Excellence

Copyright © 1995 by The American National Red Cross

All rights reserved. No part of this publication may be repro-
duced, stored in a retrieval system, or transmitted in any
form or by any means, electronic, mechanical, photocopying,
recording, or otherwise, without prior written permission from
the publisher.

This participant's textbook is an integral part of American
Red Cross training. By itself, it does not constitute complete
and comprehensive training.

Printed in the United States of America.

Composition by Graphic World, Inc.
Printing/binding by Danner Press

Mosby Lifeline
Mosby–Year Book, Inc.
11830 Westline Industrial Drive
St. Louis, MO 63146

Library of Congress Cataloging-in-Publication Data

Head lifeguard / American Red Cross.
       p. cm.
     Includes bibliographical reference and index.
     ISBN 0-8016-7554-5
     1. Lifeguards—Training of. 2. Life-saving. I. American Red
Cross.
GV838.74.H43   1994
797' .20089—dc20

94-21365
CIP

       95 96 97 / 9 8 7 6 5 4 3 2

ACKNOWLEDGMENTS

This manual was developed and produced through the combined effort of the American Red Cross and the Mosby-Year Book Publishing Company. Without the commitment to excellence of both paid and volunteer staff, this manual could not have been created.

The Health and Safety Program Development team at American Red Cross national headquarters responsible for designing and writing this book included: Lawrence D. Newell, Ed.D. NREMT-P, Manager; Rhonda Starr, Senior Associate; Martha F. Beshers, Bruce Carney, M.A. Ed., Thomas J.S. Edwards, Ph.D., Michael Espino, Marian F.H. Kirk, Jose V. Salazar, M.P.H., and Paul Stearns, Associates; Mary F. Baudo, Lori Compton, Michael Giles, Jr., and Patricia Appleford Terrell, Analysts. Administrative support was provided by Erika Miller and Elizabeth Taylor.

The following American Red Cross national headquarters Health and Safety paid and volunteer staff provided guidance and review: Ray Cranston, Program Development Volunteer Chairman; Karen White, Associate, Operations; and Cathy Brennan, Marketing Specialist.

The Mosby-Year Book Editorial and Production team included: Richard Weimer and Claire Merrick, Executive Editors; Jennifer Roe, John Probst, and Ross Goldberg, Assistant Editors; Colleen Foley, Editorial Assistant; Carol Sullivan Wiseman, Project Manager; Shannon Canty, Senior Production Editor; Kay Kramer, Director of Art & Design; Sheilah Barrett and Liz Fett, Designers; Jerry Wood, Director of Manufacturing; Theresa Fuchs, Manufacturing Supervisor; and Patricia Stinecipher, Special Product Manager.

Special thanks go to Tom Lochhaas, ABD, Developmental Editor; Carol Fuchs, M.A., M.P.W., Joseph Matthews, Daniel Cima, Vincent Knaus, Jeanette Ortiz Osorio, Mark Wieland, and Nick Caloyianis, Photographers; Harriet Kastarsis and Associates, Rolin Graphics, and Scott Hull and Associates, Illustrators; and to Donald K. Vardell, Jr., M.S., Aquatics Coordinator, Office of Recreation, University of Tennessee, Knoxville, Tennessee, for his assistance as an external writer and reviewer.

Guidance, writing, and review were also provided by members of the American Red Cross Lifeguard Advisory Group:

Michael C. Giles, Sr.
Advisory Group Chair Aquatics Director
  and Risk Manager, Recreation Sports
A Division of Student Affairs
The University of Southern Mississippi
Hattiesburg, Mississippi

Charles Bittenbring
Division Manager
Fairfax County Park Authority
Fairfax, Virginia

Robert L. Burhans, R.S.
Chief Sanitarian, Bureau of Community Sanitation and
  Food Protection
New York State Department of Health
Albany, New York

Molly A. Casey, M.S.
Director, Safety Services
American Red Cross
Metropolitan Atlanta Chapter
Atlanta, Georgia

Gerald DeMers, Ph.D.
Associate Professor and Director, Aquatic Program
Physical Education and Kinesiology Department
California Polytechnic State University
San Luis Obispo, California

Julie J. Good
Leisure Service Department
University of New Mexico
Albuquerque, New Mexico

Jerry Huey
Field Representative, Health and Safety Services
American Red Cross
Southeastern Michigan Chapter
Detroit, Michigan

Charles Kunsman, M.S.Ed.
Aquatic Manager, Ocasek Natatorium
University of Akron
Akron, Ohio

James P. Morgan
Director of Parks and Recreation
City of Lincoln
Lincoln, Nebraska

Frank Pia
Former Chief Lifeguard
Orchard Beach
Bronx, New York
Former Supervising Chief Lifeguard
Bronx, New York

Judith Sperling
Manager and Aquatics Director
Department of Cultural and Recreational Affairs
University of California Los Angeles
Los Angeles, California

Margaret Sweeney-Fedders
Assistant Director of Safety
American Red Cross
Dayton Area Chapter
Dayton, Ohio

Kim Tyson
Aquatic Safety Lecturer
Department of Kinesiology
University of Texas
Austin, Texas

Thomas C. Werts
Recreation Specialist
Walt Disney World Co.
Orlando, Florida

External review was provided by the following individuals:

Tom Griffiths, Ed.D.
Director of Aquatics
The Pennsylvania State University
University Park, Pennsylvania

Harriet J. Helmer
Aquatic Consultant
Sun Mountain Enterprises
Golden, Colorado

Newton Jackson
Department of Physical Education
Howard University
Washington, DC

Ron Morrow
Director of Physical Education
Davidson College
Davidson, North Carolina

Fontaine Piper, Ph.D.
Director and Associate Professor
Biomechanics/Motor Learning Laboratory
Northeast Missouri State University
Kirksville, Missouri

William A. Rich
Aquatics Director
Milander Pool
City of Hialeah, Florida

Thomas A. Bates, CLP, EMT-B
Aquatics Manager, Chinn Aquatics and Fitness Center
Prince William County Park Authority
Prince William, Virginia

SPECIAL ACKNOWLEDGMENTS

The American Red Cross would like to thank the following individuals and facilities who provided talent and locations for much of the photography in this book:

Gary Adelhardt
Sandy Point State Park
Annapolis, MD

Ashburn Village Sports Pavillion
Ashburn, VA

Thomas A. Bates
Prince William County Park Authority
Prince William, Virginia

Melissa Johnson and Jean Skinner
Fairfax County Park Authority
South Run Recreation Center
Fairfax, Virginia

Janis Carley
Cape Coral Yacht Club
Sun Splash Family Waterpark
Cape Coral, Florida

Dale and Barbara Dohner
Camp Oneka
Wayne, Pennsylvania

Pat Harrison Waterway District
Flint Creek
Wiggins, Mississippi

Scot Hunsaker
Councilman, Hunsaker & Associates
St. Louis, Missouri

Gary Peterson
Belle Isle Beach
Detroit Park and Recreation
Detroit, Michigan

Sterling Volunteer Rescue Squad
Sterling, Virginia

Steve Wyatt
Rolling Hills Water Park
Ypsilanti, Michigan

Acknowledgments

AAA Ambulance Service
Hattiesburg, Mississippi

Baltimore County Parks and Recreation
Oregan Ridge Lake
Baltimore, Maryland

Fritz Cheek
Camp Copneconic
Fenton, Michigan

Concord Mews Pool
Arlington, Virginia

Greenbrier State Park
Greenbrier Lake
Boonsboro, Maryland

Gunpowder Falls State Park
Hammerman Area
Gunpowder River
Baltimore, Maryland

Metro Dade County Parks and Recreation
Miami, Florida

Oceans of Fun
Kansas City, Missouri

Reston Association and Park Recreation
Reston, Virginia

The University of Southern Mississippi
M.C. Johnson Natatorium, Recreational Sports, a Division of
    Student Affairs
Hattiesburg, Mississippi

Virginia Department of Conservation and Recreation
Lake Anna State Park
Spotsylvania, Virginia

Walt Disney World
Orlando, Florida

Washington DC Department of Recreation
Washington, DC

PREFACE

As we move towards the 21st century, the profession of lifeguarding has taken on new meaning and responsibilities. Gone are the days of sun and fun. . . present are the days of risk management and litigation. Along with the changing roles of the lifeguard has come a need for someone to work directly with both the facility management and the lifeguards. . . someone to organize and coordinate all efforts to ensure patron safety. . .someone to provide leadership. This someone is the HEAD LIFEGUARD.

Head lifeguards must balance legal concerns and risk management with what is practical and workable at their facility. They must build a solid lifeguard team through selection, training, supervision, and evaluation. They often must also bridge the lifeguard-patron relationship which, at times, may be challenging. To carry out all of these responsibilities requires individuals with unique talents and specific training.

The American Red Cross has recognized this need, and developed both a program and a textbook specific for head lifeguards. Both the program and the textbook allow head lifeguard candidates to gain and improve the skills they will need to meet the rapidly expanding and changing aquatics environment and the demanding public. They will also become better equipped to assume the leadership role necessary to build a solid lifeguard team and ensure the safety of all who enjoy the water.

CONTENTS

HOW TO USE THIS TEXTBOOK

TEXTBOOK

This textbook has been designed to help you learn and understand the material it presents. It includes the following features:

Objectives

At the beginning of each chapter is a list of objectives. Read these objectives carefully and refer back to them from time to time as you read the chapter. The objectives describe what you should know after reading the chapter.

Key Terms

At the beginning of each chapter is a list of defined key terms that you need to know to understand chapter content. In the chapter, key terms are printed in bold italics the first time they are defined or explained.

Sidebars

Feature articles called sidebars enhance the information in the main body of the text. They appear in most chapters. They present a variety of material ranging from historical information and accounts of actual events to everyday application of the information presented in the main body of the text. If you are participating in the American Red Cross Head Lifeguard course, you will not be tested on any information presented in these sidebars as part of the course completion requirements.

Study Questions

Study questions appear at the end of each chapter. They are designed to help you understand and remember the material you have read in the chapter. Answering these questions will help you evaluate your progress and prepare for the final written examination if you are participating in the American Red Cross Head Lifeguard course. Answer them after you have read the chapter. To reinforce learning, some of the study questions have more than one correct answer. Discuss any questions with which you have difficulty with your instructor.

Appendixes

Appendixes, located at the end of this textbook, provide additional information on topics head lifeguards will find useful.

Glossary

The glossary includes definitions of all the key terms and of other words in the text that may be unfamiliar. All glossary terms appear in the textbook in bold type the first time they are used or explained.

ROLES AND RESPONSIBILITIES OF THE HEAD LIFEGUARD

1

Objectives

After reading this chapter, you should be able to—

1. List five leadership characteristics necessary for a head lifeguard.
2. Explain the responsibilities of a head lifeguard and the three categories into which they fall.
3. Define the key terms for this chapter.

Key Terms

Facility manager: The person who oversees an aquatic facility's operation, which may include staffing, maintenance, and financial operation.

Head lifeguard: A lifeguard in a supervisory position in the facility's chain of command.

Lifeguard team: Two or more lifeguards, including the head lifeguard as team leader, who work and interact as a group.

INTRODUCTION

Congratulations! You are about to become a *head lifeguard* (Fig. 1-1). Promotion to the position of head lifeguard is exciting and challenging. Yet you may feel anxious or unsure of how you will handle the additional responsibilities. This textbook will help you adapt to your new role on the lifeguard team.

One of the first things you will notice as you start working as a head lifeguard is that you have a new view of the lifeguard operation. Your first challenge as a head lifeguard is to take charge of the *lifeguard team* (Fig. 1-2). You may struggle to find the right balance without being too timid or bossy with your lifeguards. You will learn to be assertive in asking lifeguards to fulfill their primary duties.

Your leadership position in the daily lifeguard operation means making decisions and leading meetings. Listen with an open mind to the opinions of all your lifeguards, even those you do not agree with. Work to help everyone feel a part of the team. Your leadership is one of the key elements in establishing a climate of safety at your facility.

Another important task of the head lifeguard is to help lifeguards clearly understand their job in the facility. After explaining what their duties and responsibilities are, help them understand how these responsibilities are essential for the facility's operation.

You also want to build a good relationship with your supervisor. Working as a colleague with your supervisor helps you become a more mature and competent member of the management team. Talk with your supervisor to learn how he or she wants to be involved in your work issues. Good communication with your supervisor helps you understand what part you play in the overall structure of your organization.

Where you fit in the **chain of command** depends on your facility (Fig. 1-3). Typically, as head lifeguard you are at a middle level in the facility's chain of command. The *facility manager* is in charge of the entire facility's operations, including lifeguarding, but you are in direct charge of the lifeguard team (Fig. 1-4). In some small facilities, the head lifeguard may also be the facility manager. Talk to your supervisor to be sure you understand exactly where you fit in your facility's chain of command.

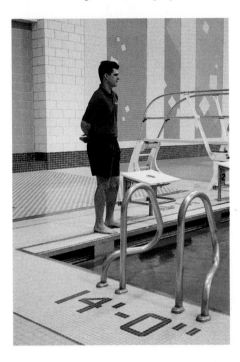

figure 1-1 *The job of head lifeguard can be exciting and challenging.*

figure 1-2 *"Taking Charge of the Lifeguard Team."*

figure 1-3 *An example of a chain of command for an aquatic facility.*

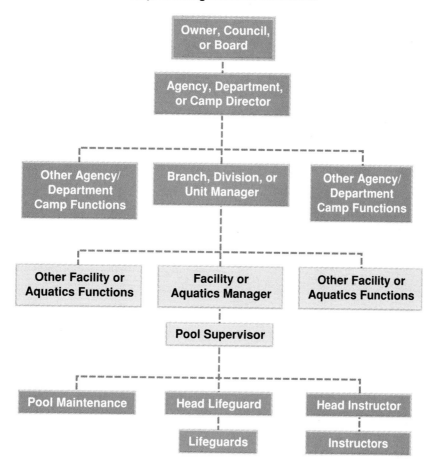

SAMPLE OF GENERIC
ORGANIZATION CHART

Representing Chain of Command

Owner, Council, or Board

Agency, Department, or Camp Director

Other Agency/ Department Camp Functions

Branch, Division, or Unit Manager

Other Agency/ Department Camp Functions

Other Facility or Aquatics Functions

Facility or Aquatics Manager

Other Facility or Aquatics Functions

Pool Supervisor

Pool Maintenance

Head Lifeguard

Head Instructor

Lifeguards

Instructors

figure 1-4 *The lifeguard team consists of the head life-guard and lifeguards.*

CHARACTERISTICS OF A HEAD LIFEGUARD

Not everyone wants to be—or can be—a head lifeguard. Clearly it's an important job with significant responsibilities. Having been an effective lifeguard does not guarantee you will be an effective head lifeguard; you need certain characteristics to take on the additional responsibilities.

In Chapter 4, you learn the characteristics to look for when you help management select lifeguards to hire. These include reliability, a positive attitude, and courtesy and consistency, in addition to rescue, first aid, and CPR skills. As head lifeguard, you need all these skills and characteristics too, but your leadership role requires additional characteristics such as the following:

- The ability to lead others, to command respect, and to motivate others
- Problem-solving and decision-making skills
- Self-confidence and initiative
- **Interpersonal** and "people management" skills
- A professional attitude and appearance

RESPONSIBILITIES

As head lifeguard, your responsibilities fall into three general categories:

- *Ensuring the safety of both the lifeguard team and facility patrons.* This includes identifying and correcting hazards that may compromise staff's or patrons' safety and educating patrons about your facility's rules and regulations. This also means being able to develop and write **emergency action plans.** It may also mean handling problem situations with uncooperative or even violent patrons.
- *Supervising and training lifeguarding staff.* This includes testing and interviewing prospective lifeguard applicants, planning and providing job-related training, and providing and scheduling staff to meet the facility's needs. In your leadership role on the lifeguard team, you are also responsible for problem solving, delegating responsibility, and improving staff performance; communicating and interacting with the lifeguard team and facility patrons; and effectively serving as a **liaison** between your supervisor and the lifeguard team.
- *Supervising the safety inspection, general care, and cleaning of the facility.* This includes the maintenance and minor repair of equipment and reporting any unsafe conditions and equipment to the facility manager immediately.

The head lifeguard job description lists other specific responsibilities. From the chapters in this book and your head lifeguard training, you will learn the skills for managing all these responsibilities effectively. The information in this book is universal and can be applied in any aquatic environment.

Sample Job Description for a Head Lifeguard

Job Title:	Head Lifeguard
Job Description:	Responsible for managing daily pool operations including, but not limited to, supervising lifeguard staff, maintaining the facility, planning and conducting in-service training for staff, and performing lifeguarding duties.

Minimum Qualifications: Certification in the following:
- American Red Cross Lifeguard Training
- American Red Cross Waterpark Lifeguarding for waterpark positions
- American Red Cross Waterfront Lifeguarding for waterfront positions
- American Red Cross Head Lifeguard
- American Red Cross Community First Aid and Safety
- American Red Cross CPR for the Professional Rescuer

The following certifications are preferred:
- American Red Cross Lifeguarding Instructor
- American Red Cross CPR for the Professional Rescuer Instructor
- Pool Operator (Local, state, or nationally-recognized certification)

Knowledge and Skills:
- Thorough knowledge and application of lifeguarding rescue techniques
- The ability to instruct, assign, supervise, and evaluate lifeguarding staff in the performance of their duties
- Knowledge of the principles and practices of facility rules, policies, and procedures
- Leadership qualities and public relations skills

Experience:
- Must have a minimum of one season or 6 months' lifeguarding experience
- Supervisory experience preferred

General Duties:
- Responsible for the safety of the facility patrons
- Responsible for the supervision of the lifeguarding staff
- Enforces all of the facility's policies, rules, and regulations
- Responds to patron inquiries and concerns
- Supervises the general care and cleaning of the facility and the maintenance and minor repair of equipment
- Inspects the facility on a daily schedule and reports any unsafe conditions and equipment to the facility manager immediately
- Maintains records, reports, and information regarding the following: hourly patron attendance, water chemistry, daily weather conditions, and incidents
- Plans and provides for the preseason and in-service training of the lifeguard staff
- Schedules lifeguard staff
- Performs lifeguard duties
- Carries out additional duties as assigned by the facility manager

Responsible to: Pool (Facility) Manager, Aquatics Director, Aquatics Supervisor, or Aquatics Superintendent

These three areas of responsibility are all related through a focus on **risk management.** In general, risk management involves everything you, management, and lifeguards do to make sure that everyone is as safe as possible in the facility and that any problem is handled as effectively as possible. In the next chapter, you will learn more about the specifics of risk management. As you continue with other chapters and learn other specific responsibilities of the head lifeguard, remember that risk management is an underlying factor behind everything you do with the whole **safety team** (Fig. 1-5).

figure 1-5 *The safety team.*

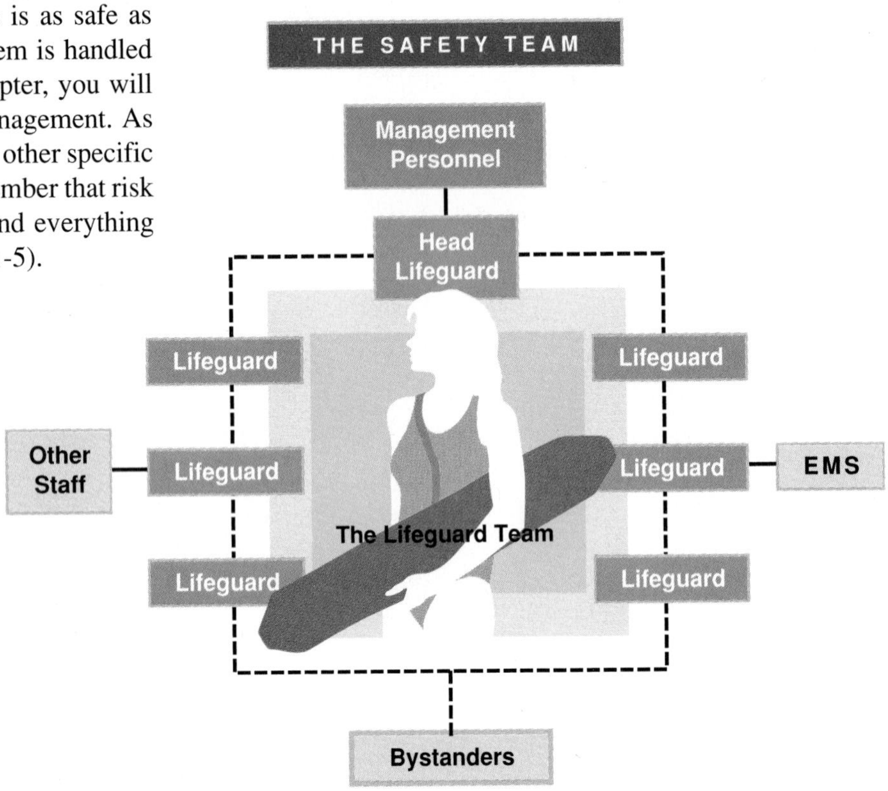

THE SAFETY TEAM

Management Personnel

Head Lifeguard

Lifeguard   Lifeguard

Other Staff   Lifeguard   The Lifeguard Team   Lifeguard   EMS

Lifeguard   Lifeguard

Bystanders

STUDY QUESTIONS

Circle the letter of the best answer or answers.

1. Which of the following would not be considered a challenge or task for the head lifeguard?
   a) Take charge of the lifeguard team.
   b) Be sure the facility is clean at all times.
   c) Give lifeguards a clear understanding of their responsibilities.
   d) Build a good working relationship with your supervisor.

2. Which of the following leadership characteristics are necessary for head lifeguards?
   a) Ability to lead others.
   b) Reliability.
   c) Problem solving and decision-making skills.
   d) First aid and CPR skills.
   e) People management skills.

3. The head lifeguard's responsibilities include which of the following categories?
   a) Ensure the safety of both the lifeguard team and the facility patrons.
   b) Supervise and train the lifeguarding staff.
   c) Hire facility staff other than lifeguards.
   d) Supervise the safety inspections, general care and cleaning of the facility, and maintenance and minor repair of equipment.

4. Everything that the head lifeguard, management, and the lifeguard team do to maintain the highest possible level of safety is called _____.
   a) Problem solving.
   b) Risk management.
   c) Safety control.
   d) Safety management.

See answers to study questions on p. 120.

MINIMIZING RISKS

2

Objectives

After reading this chapter, you should be able to—

1. Describe nine legal considerations for head lifeguards.
2. List at least six components of proper supervision that could measure a head lifeguard's standard of care.
3. Describe the four components of negligence.
4. List five reasons for keeping records and reports.
5. List the four typical components of a risk-management process.
6. List at least five categories of potential risk at an aquatic facility.
7. Define the key terms for this chapter.

Key Terms

Abandonment: Ending care of an ill or injured person without obtaining the person's consent or ensuring that someone with equal or greater training continues that care.

Confidentiality: Protecting a victim's privacy by not revealing any personal information you learn about the victim except to law enforcement personnel or EMS personnel caring for the victim.

Consent: Permission from an ill or injured person to give care.

Duty to act: A legal responsibility to provide a reasonable standard of care, as may be required by case law, statute, or job description.

Lawsuit: A legal procedure for settling a dispute.

Negligence: The failure to provide the level (standard) of care a person of similar training would provide, thereby resulting in harm to another.

Risk management: Identifying and eliminating or minimizing dangerous conditions that can cause injury and financial loss.

Standard of care: The minimum standard and level of care expected of a head lifeguard.

INTRODUCTION

The management of an aquatic facility is responsible for providing an environment that is as risk-free as possible for patrons at the facility. One very important aspect of risk management is injury prevention, which is discussed in Chapter 3. Management is also responsible for minimizing two other kinds of risk—risk to the assets of the facility and risk of legal action against the facility and staff. Managing risk involves a process of identifying and evaluating the particular risks at a facility and then using various strategies to address them. The risk management information contained in this chapter is general and designed only to acquaint you with basic risk management concepts. Your facility should have its own risk management program. It is your responsibility to become familiar with the portions of the program that are applicable to your position.

Minimizing the risk of legal action includes making lifeguards aware of legal considerations involved in the job. As a head lifeguard, you are legally responsible for your actions and those of your lifeguards. You may be responsible if a lifeguard acts incorrectly because he or she lacks training or misunderstands facility policies and procedures. When you become a head lifeguard, you accept some management responsibilities. You must fulfill the duties of the head lifeguard position, especially to provide as safe a facility as possible for the patrons.

Because your actions are judged against **industry standards,** you must be able to provide appropriate care for patrons when needed. Maintaining your certifications with national organizations, such as the American Red Cross, helps keep you well informed and well trained, but you must also meet your particular job responsibilities. You and your lifeguards act to minimize risks, take precautions to prevent injuries, and respond quickly to emergency situations. Following facility policies and procedures should reduce the chance of an incident occurring and, if one does occur, helps minimize its severity (Fig. 2-1).

LEGAL CONSIDERATIONS

In any job involving responsibility for others, employees are naturally concerned about the possibility of a lawsuit if something happens. A *lawsuit* is a legal procedure for settling a dispute. If your facility has a catastrophic incident involving death or disability, such as a drowning, near drowning, or spinal injury, a lawsuit may result. Understanding the legal principles involved in your responsibilities, however, can help you avoid liability. The following nine sections describe legal principles you need to understand (Fig. 2-2).

figure 2-1 *Following your facility's policies and procedures helps reduce the possibility of an incident.*

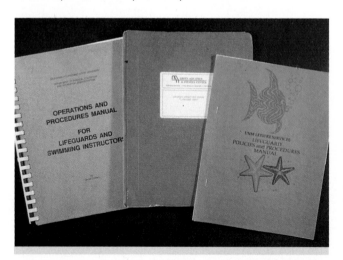

figure 2-2 *Head lifeguards should be aware of these basic legal considerations.*

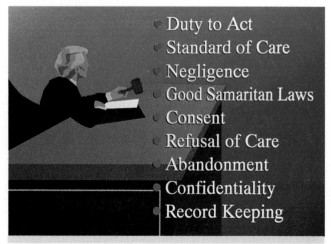

- Duty to Act
- Standard of Care
- Negligence
- Good Samaritan Laws
- Consent
- Refusal of Care
- Abandonment
- Confidentiality
- Record Keeping

Duty to act

Because of their job definition, lifeguards have a **duty to act** if an emergency occurs at the facility. The public expects lifeguards to help keep patrons safe by preventing incidents and injuries and by recognizing and responding to people in need.

As a head lifeguard, you also have a duty to act. Your job responsibilities include providing in-service training for your staff, correcting deficiencies, responding in an emergency, and supervising the care your staff provides. If you fail to fulfill these responsibilities, which you agreed to when you took the job, you could be subject to legal action. The following examples describe some steps you should take as part of overseeing lifeguards:

- Test their rescue skills.
- Conduct training in the use of all equipment specific to your facility.
- Conduct training on emergency action plans, including simulated responses to patrons in distress, spinal injuries on the deck or in locker rooms, poisonous gas leaks, facility evacuation, and patron disturbances.
- Conduct training in policies and procedures dealing with special groups using your facility such as swim teams, summer camps, adaptive aquatics, water exercise, and others.

Standard of care

The public expects a certain **standard of care** from lifeguards who look out for their well-being in the aquatic facility (Fig. 2-3). This standard of care is based on training guidelines developed by national lifeguard training organizations, such as the American Red Cross, and on state or local laws or regulations.

Your actions as a head lifeguard should be at the same level as those of other trained head lifeguards in similar situations. In a lawsuit, a court would determine whether you or your staff were negligent by not following the standards of care. The court would ask whether a reasonable and prudent person using current professional practices would have acted in the same manner under the same circumstances. For head lifeguards, this applies not only to their actions but also to the actions of the lifeguarding staff they supervise. In this case, the standard includes proper supervision by the head lifeguard. This standard of care includes whether—

- Adequate supervision is present.
- The supervisor is aware of a dangerous condition.
- All staff have proper training or certification.
- Policies and procedures are understood and enforced.
- Supervisor(s), lifeguards, and patrons communicate appropriately.
- Patrons understand and adhere to safety practices.
- Supervisor(s) and staff understand limits for participants in specific activities.
- Adequate instructions and appropriate skill progressions are given in aquatic activity classes.
- Adequate warnings of dangers are given (danger signs posted), and protective devices (life jackets) are used as required.
- Equipment and the facility are checked appropriately.

figure 2-3 *Patrons expect the lifeguard to look out for their well-being while swimming.*

Case Study #1

A 21-year-old college student becomes a head lifeguard at a local municipal pool for the summer. He has been a lifeguard at similar facilities for 3 years. He is thoroughly oriented to his new position by his supervisor. Detailed lesson plans and time schedules for staff in-service training are provided. He acknowledges his responsibility to conduct this staff training when he accepts the position. Unfortunately, he departs from the written policies and procedures and does not provide this training, believing it is unnecessary. Later that summer, a child is rescued from the bottom of the pool, but the lifeguards delay their initial emergency care and are slow to contact EMS personnel. These delays are believed to have contributed to the death of the child. The appropriate prompt steps are well established in the emergency action plan and in additional materials presented during in-service training, but the head lifeguard did not present this training to the lifeguards. Has this head lifeguard failed to uphold a standard of care expected of him? Did his failure result in harm to another person?

Negligence

Negligence is the failure to do what a reasonably careful and responsible person would do in the same or similar circumstances or doing something that a careful and prudent person would not have done. Negligence is a failure to act in accordance with the standard of care.

Four components must be present for anyone to be guilty of negligence:

- The person has a *duty*
- The person's actions were a *breach of duty* (infraction or violation of a law, obligation, or standard)
- The breach was the *cause* of harm
- *Damage* (harm) to another resulted

As head lifeguard, you have a duty to oversee staff and respond to emergencies in a professional manner, following policies and procedures. If you fail in this duty, then you commit a **breach of duty.** Neglecting this duty may cause an injury or cause improper care to be given, resulting in harm to a patron.

The following scenario illustrates a case of possible negligence:

A 14-year-old girl is injured in shallow water when a large man jumps from the deck and lands on her as she is surfacing. Bystanders report the incident to the lifeguard, who then enters the water to assist. The head lifeguard comes to the deck nearby. The girl has a cut on her forehead and complains of dizziness and back pain. The head lifeguard supervising the actions of the lifeguard urges the injured girl to walk to the nearest ladder and climb out, although no immediate danger threatens. This movement causes the girl to experience severe pain, and she suddenly loses feeling in her legs and collapses. In this case, the head lifeguard may be negligent because he or she did not follow the reasonable standard of care for immobilizing the patron on a backboard.

Good Samaritan laws

Most states have **Good Samaritan laws** to protect people who provide emergency care. These laws differ somewhat from state to state but generally help protect you and your staff when you act in good faith and within the scope of your training and are not negligent. Some Good Samaritan laws, however, do not provide coverage for individuals who have a duty to respond. For this reason, it is important that you know the degree to which your state's Good Samaritan laws will help protect you and your staff.

Consent

Before you can provide care for an ill or injured patron, you or your lifeguards must obtain his or her *consent.* Usually, the patron should state clearly that he or she gives permission for you to provide care. When asking for consent, you should tell the patron—

- Your level of training.
- What you think may be wrong.
- What you plan to do.

With this information, the patron can grant his or her **informed consent** for care. Someone who is unconscious, confused, or seriously ill or injured (such as in a near drowning) may not be able to grant consent. In these cases the law assumes the patron would give consent if he or she were able to do so. This is called **implied consent.** When a parent or guardian is not present, you also have implied consent for minors who obviously need emergency assistance.

Refusal of care

Some ill or injured persons may refuse the care you offer. Even if the person seems seriously injured, you must honor this **refusal of care.** Try to convince the person of the need for care. Request that the person at least allow someone more highly trained, such as EMS personnel, to evaluate the situation. Make it clear that you are not refusing to care for or abandoning this person. Ask someone else, such as a lifeguard, to witness the person's refusal and document it. Your facility may have a form for documenting a patron's refusal.

Abandonment

Once you or your lifeguards are providing care to a patron, you are obligated to continue or complete the care. In a serious situation, such as with a nonbreathing victim, you are legally obligated to continue rescue breathing until you are relieved by someone with equal or higher training, such as EMS personnel. If you stop your care before that point, you can be legally responsible for the *abandonment* of a person in need.

Confidentiality

Any time you or your staff care for an ill or injured person, you may learn information about the person, such as about medical conditions, physical problems, and medications taken. *Confidentiality* protects the victim's right to privacy by not revealing information learned about the victim. Reporters or attorneys may ask questions. Never discuss the victim or the care given with anyone except law enforcement or EMS personnel (Fig. 2-4).

Case Study #2

An 8-year-old child enters the water from a 1-meter board and swims to the bottom of the pool. She does not surface. A lifeguard makes a rescue and with the assistance of other lifeguards removes the child from the water. On the pool deck, it becomes clear that the child is having a seizure. The lifeguards place her on her side to help keep her airway clear. Later she vomits but otherwise appears to be fine once the seizure has passed.

As head lifeguard, you did not immediately notify EMS personnel because you wanted to see first whether she needed their help. The camp counselor who brought the child to the pool in a group now comes up to you and says that the child is prone to seizures, but she appears to be OK now and the group is leaving. The counselor wants to take the child with the others, and you let her go.

You first failed to have your staff call 9-1-1, and then you failed to advise the counselor that anyone who has a seizure in the water should be evaluated by more advanced medical personnel. Later that day, the child is hospitalized for complications from the near-drowning incident. Do you think the child's parents have grounds for legal action against you, your staff, or the facility?

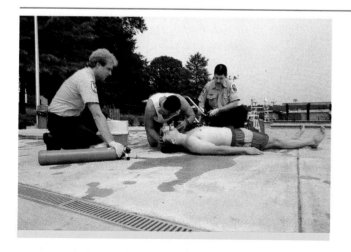

figure 2-4 *Discuss the care given to a victim only with law enforcement or EMS personnel.*

Record keeping

Many aquatic facilities require records and reports to be kept. Accuracy in record keeping is essential for effective facility management. Consider this saying: "If it is not written down, it did not happen." Use this as a guideline for the need for proper documentation.

In most facilities, you document daily operation and activities in a daily log that is kept as a running narrative. (See Appendix A for a sample daily log.) Enter in the log general comments about opening and closing times, conditions of the facility, personnel, and equipment. Also include changes in scheduling due to illness or emergency, any discipline problems, and routine maintenance. Note all incidents and injuries, and refer to the specific record for that incident or injury. You or management may later use this information to evaluate the total facility, personnel performances, and day-to-day operations.

In general the larger the facility and management structure, the more records and reports are needed. Each facility has its own forms and set number of copies required of each. Although reporting systems differ among facilities, the content of the forms is usually similar.

Be thoroughly familiar with each record or report form used at your facility. As the head lifeguard, you may be required to explain the forms and guide others in their use. Some of these forms are—

- Preemployment forms.
- Working reports.
- Incident report forms.
- In-service training records.
- Lifeguard evaluation forms.

The purposes of records and reports include the following:

- To provide information for decisions about equipment, schedules, personnel, procedural changes, and facility improvements
- To provide information for research on the causes and prevention of injuries and fatalities
- To provide a basis for budget recommendations and future expenditures, along with their justification to management
- To comply with state and local laws requiring specific records about sanitation and maintenance
- To document incidents and injuries for use in facility risk-management programs, compliance with laws, and possible legal actions

You and your lifeguard team need to complete records and reports accurately and thoroughly. All records and reports must be signed, dated, filed, and kept in accordance with the facility's record keeping policies. Your facility may also require copies of certain reports to be forwarded to others for safe-keeping.

Case Study #3

As head lifeguard, you know that written procedures at your outdoor pool require, as they have for the past 3 years, that at least 3 lifeguards (2 in lifeguard chairs and 1 roving) be stationed at all times. One afternoon, when the temperature rises above 100 degrees F, you decide not to station the roving lifeguard at the shallow end because it feels too hot to be walking on the deck.

A 4-year-old child nearly drowns in the 4-foot-deep part of the pool, an area normally supervised by the roving lifeguard. The child is hospitalized and has long-term disabilities as the result of the submersion. Did your deviation from established procedures contribute to this incident? Do you think the child's parents have grounds for legal action against you and the facility?

RISK MANAGEMENT

The term *risk management* generally describes management's responsibility and effort to protect itself and its **assets** against possible loss. Assets include the aquatic facility and the revenue it generates. Risk-management activities are typically done by senior management personnel, a professional risk manager, and an **insurance underwriter.** To develop an effective risk-management plan, this group needs input from many sources, including you and your lifeguard team.

Aquatic facilities by their nature are hazardous environments. A hazard means there is always the possibility of injury. Even a clear, shallow water pool 3 feet deep is hazardous if the person using it is only 3 feet tall. Beyond the obvious hazards of an aquatic environment are the risks inherent in various water activities. You can apply basic risk-management principles, however, to help reduce or eliminate risks at your facility.

A typical risk-management process has four components:

- Identify the risks.
- Evaluate the risks.
- Select methods to address the risks.
- Implement procedures to help protect against loss.

Identifying risks

Begin by surveying your facility. As you inspect the facility, talk with lifeguards about what risks they may feel are present. Think about all the emergency situations that could occur. Consider the following categories:

- Equipment (rescue tube, backboard, oxygen, boat)
- Structures (diving boards, play structures)
- Environment (currents, storms, fog, lightning)
- Evacuation (poisonous gas leak, fire, storm)
- Communications (telephones, radio, signals)
- Care (initial medical care for near-drowning victims and spinal injuries)
- Crowd control (spectators, theft)
- Rescue (single or multiple victims, submerged or on the surface)
- After hours (security, trespassing)

Be sure to know the state or local laws, standards, and guidelines that apply to your facility. Identifying risks is not a one-time process. Instead, make this an ongoing process at your facility.

Evaluating risks

You can evaluate the likelihood and severity of risks in several ways. While some risks could lead to serious physical or financial loss, others may be less serious but more likely to occur. Evaluate previous facility records and reports. Analyze past emergencies, how staff responded, and the results of their actions. This information can help you develop a better picture of the risks of particular aquatic activities, facility structures, or facility areas.

Selecting methods to address risks

Once you have identified and evaluated risks, facility management needs to decide what to do about them. Is a risk so great that it must be completely eliminated? This is true, for example, with a 1-meter springboard positioned where the water is not deep enough or the distance in front or to the sides of the board is inadequate for safe diving (Fig. 2-5).

With some risks, facility management may decide to accept the risk, reduce it, or transfer it to another party. Management often accepts relatively routine risks, such as the chance of a child falling when running on the deck, even though signs are posted and rules enforced that prohibit running. Risk reduction is a primary part of risk management. Reducing risk often means analyzing procedures and evaluating aspects of the facility operation, such as those that follow, to reduce the frequency and magnitude of incidents and injuries:

- Competence and training of personnel
- Activities offered and how they are supervised
- Warning signs
- Records and reports
- Facility maintenance

figure 2-5 *Once risks have been identified and evaluated, you need to decide what to do about them.*

Transferring a risk means moving the financial and other liability risks from one organization to another. This is done when risks cannot be completely eliminated and could have expensive consequences even when reduced. Examples are purchasing insurance for property damage, **liability insurance** in case of negligence by any facility staff member, accident insurance for patrons' medical expenses for accidents occurring on the premises, and **workers' compensation** for employees' medical expenses.

Risks can also be transferred by contractors with a professional group to provide specific services. For example, a facility may contract with a local dive shop with certified instructors to teach SCUBA courses at the facility during hours the facility is not normally open. Many of the risks associated with a course in SCUBA diving may therefore be transferred from the facility to the dive shop through specific legal terms in the contract that make the dive shop responsible for liability claims from the course.

Implementing procedures

In the final phase of the risk-management process, operational procedures may be developed and written by the facility to help management and staff carry out changes for eliminating, reducing, or transferring risks in your facility. Such procedures may include hiring new personnel for additional job functions, rehearsing emergency action plans through in-service training, documenting all training and incidents at the facility, and continually evaluating the results of emergency responses.

Your involvement in the four components of the risk-management process helps the facility manager better minimize risks at your facility.

SUMMARY

Your responsibilities as head lifeguard are to meet the standards of care for your profession. Even when you perform your responsibilities exactly as trained, someone who is injured in your facility may have the legal right to file a lawsuit to challenge whether you performed your duties correctly. In such a case, a court may judge what you did or did not do in comparison with the current standard of care. The guidelines presented in this chapter can help you better understand your legal obligations and how to manage your risks and the risks for others working with you. Recognizing these risks and establishing practices to deal with them means you will be acting in an appropriate professional manner as a head lifeguard.

STUDY QUESTIONS

Circle the letter of the best answer or answers.

1. The failure to exercise reasonable and ordinary care is called—
   a) Abandonment.
   b) Standard of care.
   c) Duty to act.
   d) Negligence.
   e) Confidentiality.

2. To determine whether proper supervision was provided when an injury occurred, a standard of care for a head lifeguard would include which of the following?
   a) The staff had proper training.
   b) The supervisor was aware of a dangerous condition.
   c) Patrons understood and adhered to safety practices.
   d) Equipment and the facility were checked appropriately.
   e) The patron granted his or her informed consent to receive care.
   f) Policies and procedures were understood and enforced.
   g) Adequate supervision was given.

3. Which of the following components must be present for a lawsuit charging negligence to be successful?
   a) Duty
   b) Consent
   c) Breach
   d) Abandonment
   e) Cause
   f) Damage

4. The law assumes that a person who is unconscious, confused, or seriously ill or injured would grant consent to receive care if he or she were able to do so. This is termed—
   a) Refusal of care.
   b) Implied consent.
   c) Informed consent.
   d) Exclusive consent.

5. In an aquatic facility, records and reports should be kept to—
   a) Provide information for research as to causes and prevention of injuries and fatalities.
   b) Provide information for decisions about equipment, schedules, personnel, procedural changes, and improvements.
   c) Document incidents and injuries.
   d) Comply with state and local laws that require specific information about sanitation and maintenance.
   e) Justify budget recommendations and future expenditures to management.

6. The components of the risk-management process include—
   a) Providing documentation of all incidents.
   b) Identifing the risks.
   c) Selecting methods to address the risks.
   d) Evaluating the risks.
   e) Implementing procedures to help protect against loss.
   f) Duty to act.

7. Which of the following categories should be considered as possible sources of risks at an aquatic facility?
   a) Equipment
   b) Environment
   c) In-service training
   d) Crowd control
   e) Structures
   f) Evacuation

8. Which aspects of facility operations should be evaluated to help reduce the number and seriousness of incidents and injuries?
   a) Activities offered and how they are supervised
   b) Facility maintenance
   c) Warning signs
   d) Competence and training of staff

See answers to study questions on page 120.

AQUATIC INJURY PREVENTION

3

Objectives

After reading this chapter, you should be able to—

1. Explain how a head lifeguard can help protect patrons from injury through communication.

2. List and describe two ways in which a facility's patron load can be controlled.

3. List four methods for developing a lifeguard schedule.

4. List seven factors that can determine the location of a lifeguard station.

5. Explain the reasons for elevated, ground-level, and boat lifeguard stations at an aquatic facility.

6. Explain the advantages and disadvantages of zone coverage and total coverage.

7. Explain the importance of rotating lifeguards during surveillance duty.

8. Explain how the five types of programs can affect patron surveillance.

9. Explain how the different types of special-use pools and structures can affect patron surveillance.

10. List four health, sanitation, and facility security items that should be included in a facility's policies and procedures manual.

11. List at least ten items that should be inspected daily in a first aid station.

12. Describe six precautions that a head lifeguard and facility management can take to help eliminate or decrease vandalism at an aquatic facility.

13. Define the key terms for this chapter.

Key Terms

Area of responsibility: The zone or area for which a lifeguard conducts surveillance.

Backup coverage: The expansion of areas of responsibility by other lifeguards that takes place when one lifeguard is taken away from his or her surveillance to perform a rescue.

Patron loads: The number of patrons that health codes permit as the maximum number that can be in a facility or a pool at one time.

Rotation: The scheduled moving of lifeguards for surveillance purposes from one lifeguard stand or other area to another.

Scanning: A visual technique used by lifeguards to properly observe and monitor patrons participating in aquatic activities.

Spas: Small pools or tubs in which people sit in rapidly circulating hot water.

Surveillance: A close watch kept over someone or something, such as patrons and the facility.

Therapy pool: A pool in a facility specifically used for medically prescribed treatment and rehabilitation.

Zones: A section or division of an area established for a specific purpose. *See also* Area of responsibility.

INTRODUCTION

When people come to an aquatic facility, they expect it to be as safe as possible. The lifeguard team under your leadership is an essential element for that safety. Your most important duty as head lifeguard is to ensure that your lifeguards implement the three aquatic injury control strategies: communication, patron surveillance, and facility surveillance. Aquatic injuries can potentially occur anywhere at any time. You must prepare the lifeguard team to help prevent these incidents. As the head lifeguard, you are responsible for the health and safety of your facility patrons.

COMMUNICATION

Communication strategies help protect patrons from injury and death. Each patron receives safety information through the posted rules and regulations that you and your lifeguards enforce. Warning signs help prevent injury by alerting patrons to dangers and requiring them to act safely (Fig. 3-1).

figure 3-1 *Warning signs help prevent injury by alerting patrons to dangers.*

Post rules and regulations at all entrances to your facility. Do not let patrons enter without seeing the rules and regulations you expect them to follow.

Do not assume, however, that all patrons will read and understand posted rules. Because age, mental ability, **literacy,** and other factors determine one's ability to read and understand, you cannot assume that rules and regulations that are clear to you are equally clear to all patrons.

Rules and regulations at your facility are usually based on health codes, local **ordinances,** and facility policies and procedures. Health codes focus on preventing disease transmission and other safety issues. For example, health codes prohibit patrons from entering the pool without showering and from swimming when they have open sores. You should review and understand your facility's copy of local health regulations.

Rules of conduct for patrons fall into two groups: general behavior expected of patrons anywhere in the facility and specific behaviors expected when using specific equipment and structures.

Be sure your lifeguards can identify and correct rule infractions without neglecting surveillance duties. They should take no more than a few seconds to correct a patron. A lifeguard on surveillance may not be able to explain a rule within a few seconds. If necessary, you should be available to explain the rationale for a rule.

It is difficult to explain the rationale for the *No Diving* rule, for example, in a few seconds. A person who asks why he or she is not allowed to dive into water that is 5 feet in depth often has, in some other place, dived into water of similar depth without being injured. You can explain that not being injured in the past is no guarantee that he or she will not be injured now or in the future.

Explain that diving from the side of a pool into shallow water is a complex skill that requires training and experience to be safe. Dives a person may have done into shallow water as a child are dangerous for him or her now because he or she is taller, weighs more, and enters the water with greater **velocity.**

Your explanation of these rules, such as no diving, may also help people avoid dangerous behavior in other settings where injuries often occur, such as backyard pools, docks, piers, streams, and quarries. Taking the time to explain the rationale for the rule may help prevent someone from later diving into shallow water somewhere else—and may save the person from spending the remainder of his or her life permanently disabled.

PATRON SURVEILLANCE

Patron loads, lifeguard-to-patron ratios, programming of activities, structures within the facility, and special-use pools are all factors you must consider in patron *surveillance.* You can identify the hazards of different activities and prevent injury. You should also plan ahead before an activity and give your lifeguarding staff information about the activity and its participants. This will help the lifeguards prepare for any emergencies.

Patron loads

Many state and local health codes have specific regulations about *patron loads.* In other cases, you and the facility manager may establish the patron load. The patron load is the maximum number of individuals allowed either in the water or in the facility at any time. You should know the patron load for your facility and the pool as stated in state and local regulations. The patron load should be posted at all entrances to the facility (Fig. 3-2).

You need a way to regulate how many patrons are in your facility to stay within the patron load. You can keep track of the number of patrons by periodically taking a head count. At many facilities, the cashier keeps track of the number of patrons entering the facility and stops admitting people when the facility reaches maximum capacity.

Staffing

Some state and local health codes specify that a certain number of lifeguards must be on duty for a given number of patrons. For example, a county health code may specify that for every 25 patrons in the water, the facility must have one lifeguard on surveillance duty. In some cases, however, state and local health codes do not specify a number of lifeguards on duty per a number of patrons. You or your management usually set this ratio through some criteria, such as the number of patrons that come to the facility at different times of day.

To determine how many lifeguards to schedule, consider participation records from past years and the nature of the activity. These records help you know how large a crowd to expect on holidays and during special events. If the patron load is large, you may need more lifeguards. If additional lifeguards are unavailable, you may have to close part of the facility.

There are also guidelines using ratios of square feet of pool surface area to number of lifeguards. For example, the Council for National Cooperation in Aquatics (CNCA) recommends one lifeguard should be on duty for every 2000 square feet of pool surface area open.

Scheduling

Scheduling is an important responsibility of most head lifeguards. It ensures adequate staff are present to supervise the activities scheduled for any given time. It also minimizes the number of changes, substitutions, and no-shows among lifeguards while promoting a sense of responsibility and commitment.

Make schedules at least 2 weeks in advance to help both the facility and lifeguards make plans. Minimize your scheduling work by using an established schedule for a period of time. You may be able to schedule months in advance if you hire staff to work specific shifts for a season or other period, such as an academic semester or quarter.

figure 3-2 *A sign indicating the patron load.*

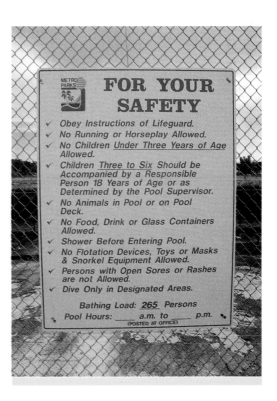

When preparing a schedule, look first at facility activities for the schedule period. Consider these factors:

- The types of programs or activities planned
- The age and skill level of the participants
- Any special uses or groups

Use your facility records to estimate the number of patrons who will be at the facility, since you don't want to overestimate or underestimate the number of lifeguards you will need.

When making schedules, remember your lifeguards are people. They have other interests and responsibilities you should acknowledge. Many lifeguards are high school or college students who need time to study. They may participate in clubs, on sports teams, or in church or other outside activities. They also need time for a social life and vacations. Work with your staff so that they can continue their other interests. This will help build teamwork, morale, and commitment to the job.

Effective methods for developing a staff schedule include the following:

- Hire staff to fill designated shifts. For example, you may have morning, evening, and weekend shifts. Staff are hired to fill specific shifts and always work those shifts.
- Post shifts that need to be filled and let staff sign up for them, then assign the shifts that aren't taken.
- Assign shifts based on set criteria or factors such as—
  - Seniority.
  - Best work record based on performance evaluations, attendance, or participation in in-service training.
  - Ability and willingness to do other jobs, such as cashiering, maintenance, and so on.
- Use a combination of these approaches. For example, you may hire staff to work weekday hours but assign the number of shifts or hours worked based on performance evaluations.

Whatever method you choose, establish a fair and uniform system and stick to it. Put the process in writing in the facility's policy and procedures manual, and give it to all staff when they are hired. It should cover how shifts are assigned, what is expected for lifeguards to get the shifts they want, what types of behavior can cause lifeguards to lose shifts, and how shifts will run (rotations, non-surveillance time and functions, reporting duty).

Be sure to schedule staff so that they can get adequate rest between shifts. A lifeguard who works the late shift one night, such as until 10 or 11 PM, should not work the early shift the next morning, such as beginning at 6 or 7 AM. A lifeguard who pulls a double shift one day should get the next day off. In addition, follow any local regulations regarding the work hours of minors.

Post schedules in a standard and conspicuous place, possibly in more than one location. A good place may be the pool office, lifeguard break room, the concession area, or by the time clock or sign-in/out logs (Fig. 3-3).

Use a set system for shift substitutions. Emphasize to your lifeguards that once a schedule is posted, they have a **contractual** agreement for services to be performed and cannot break that agreement unless an emergency arises or they follow the procedure for finding a substitute. It is often best to have lifeguards find their own substitute if they wish to change a schedule or shift. Be sure that substitutes come only from approved staff. You or your supervisor should approve and sign each change and keep signatures on file until the shift is over. Figure 3-4 is a picture of a form you can use for documenting substitutions. When lifeguards are sick or experience a true emergency, you must find a substitute.

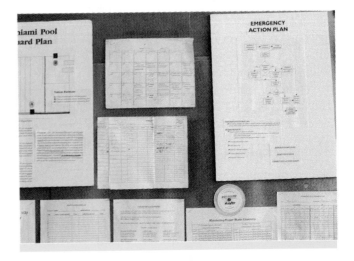

figure 3-3 *Post lifeguard schedules in a standard and conspicuous place.*

Lifeguards should report in time to be ready for their first assignment or rotation at the designated time. If a rotation begins at 3:00 PM, for example, they must arrive in time to change, review any special notes or directions for the shift, and be at the station at 3:00 PM—not just walk in the door at 3:00 PM. One way to help ensure this promptness and to help maintain knowledge and skills is to schedule staff to arrive 15 or 30 minutes before shifts begin and have an assignment during this time block each day. The assignment may be a water rescue or CPR practice, review of pool rules, or a fitness swim.

Figure 3-5, *A* and *B*, shows a sample completed schedule form. (See Appendix B for a blank copy of these forms.) Computer **software** programs can simplify the scheduling process. A program can let you enter and store information about shift availability, special needs of staff, special certifications and skills of staff, and so on. Then the computer can quickly prepare a schedule with the correct number of staff per shift and can also ensure that staff with special skills or certifications are scheduled when needed. Check with the professional recreation associations listed in Appendix C for information about scheduling programs.

Stationing lifeguards

Lifeguard surveillance may be done from the deck, the beach, or the water. The goal is to provide optimum coverage for the whole facility.

Lifeguard stands should be located where lifeguards can observe patrons easily and react quickly to any situation in their *area of responsibility.* Stands and chairs are for the use of lifeguards only. They must not be used as gymnastic or diving equipment or as storage areas for personal items of swimmers or lifeguards. Keep food, drinks, and radios off the lifeguard stands. Lifeguards should politely ask people to keep the area around the stand, and especially in front of it, clear at all times.

When determining where to locate lifeguard stations, consider the following:

- Size and shape of the facility
- Depth of the water
- Number of patrons in the facility
- Movement of the sun and wind
- Condition (clarity) of the water
- Size of the deck or dock area surrounding the water
- Type of activity, for example, recreational swimming, swimming lessons, diving

figure 3-5 *A* and *B*, *Examples of a weekly and a semester lifeguard schedule.*

Lifeguard Schedule

Week of ___3/7/94___ to ___3/13/94___

Lifeguard	Monday 7	Tuesday 8	Wednesday 9	Thursday 10	Friday 11	Saturday 12	Sunday 13	Total Hours
Tom	6-10am	6-10am	6-10am	6-10am	6-10am			20
Charlie		9:30am-2pm		9:30am-2pm		1-7pm		15
Molly	6-10am		6-10am		6-10am			12
Martha		6-10am		6-10am				8
Liz	9:30am-2pm		9:30am-2pm		9:30am-2pm			13.5
Mike E.	10am-2:30pm		10am-2:30pm		10am-2:30pm			13.5
Rhonda	2-6pm	2-6pm	2-6pm	2-6pm	2-7pm			21
Jerry	2:30-7pm		2:30-7pm		2:30-5pm			11.5
Chuck	7-9:30pm		7-9:30pm		5-9:30pm			9.5
Ray		2:30-7pm		2:30-7pm			11am-5pm	15
Mike G.		7-9:30pm		7-9:30pm		9am-1pm		9
Mary	6-9:30pm				6:30-9:30pm		11am-5pm	12.5
Judith		6-9:30pm	6-9:30pm	6-9:30pm		2-7pm		15.5
Patty		10am-2:30pm		10am-2:30pm		9am-2pm		14

figure 3-4 *An example of a lifeguard substitute form.*

Aquatic Staff Substitution Form

I, _____ will substitute for _____
   Substitute Lifeguard   Scheduled Lifeguard

on _____ , from _____ am / pm to _____ am / pm.
   Month and Day   Time   (Circle One)   Time   (Circle One)

_____   _____
Scheduled Lifeguard's Signature   Substitute Lifeguard's Signature

_____
Aquatic Manager's or Head Lifeguard's Approval

Lifeguard Schedule
Fall Semester

Times	Monday	Tuesday	Wednesday	Thursday	Friday	Saturday	Sunday
6:30-8:00am	Tom / Charlie	Martha / Larry	Tom /Charlie	Martha / Larry	Mike G / Charlie	Larry / Patty	Closed
8:00-9:00am		Jerry		Jerry			
9:00-10:00am	Molly	Rhonda	Molly	Rhonda	Molly		
10:00-11:00am						Charlie	
11:00-12:00pm	Martha		Chuck		Martha	Mary	
12:00-1:00pm		Don		Cathy			
1:00-2:00pm	Liz		Liz		Don		
2:00-3:00pm							Closed
3:00-4:00pm	Martha / Mike E.	Ray / Judith	Patty / Mike E.	Ray / Liz	Patty / Mike E.		
4:00-5:00pm							
5:00-6:30pm		Chuck		Chuck			
6:30-8:30pm	Mike G.		Mike G.		Ray		
8:30-10:20pm	Tom	Jerry	Molly	Jerry	Tom		

Not all factors apply in all facilities, and some have different conditions that affect the location of the lifeguard stations. You need to establish a system of coverage that places the lifeguards where they can provide maximum safety for the patrons.

Elevated stations. Elevated stations, such as towers, stands, or chairs, usually provide lifeguards with a better vantage point from which to scan their area of responsibility (Fig. 3-6). In facilities with large open-water areas, lifeguards may need to use binoculars. In camps, the person in the elevated station acts as a lookout or observer and directs lifeguards on the ground to swimmers who need assistance.

Some facilities require lifeguards to climb down from elevated chairs and stands rather than jump because of a hard surface beneath the chair or because the chair is located near shallow water.

Ground-level stations. In some small facilities, all lifeguards are stationed at ground or deck level. These lifeguards may be assigned to specific areas (stationary), or they may be required to move around the area (roving) (Fig. 3-7). Roving lifeguards may be needed where many swimmers are concentrated or where water depth suddenly changes, such as at the shallow-water end of a wave pool or the receiving pool at the end of a speed slide or water flume. Roving lifeguards should always carry a rescue tube.

One advantage of placing lifeguards at ground level is that they are close to patrons. This allows for more quiet and effective disciplinary actions, since the lifeguards may not have to shout or blow a whistle to attract a swimmer's attention. This advantage is usually not as important, however, as the surveillance advantages of elevated stations.

Boat stations. In open-water areas, such as camps or parks, one or two lifeguards may be stationed in a boat at the outer edges of the swimming area (Fig. 3-8). The boat should not enter the swimming area except in an emergency. The lifeguards can easily patrol deep water in a boat and reach swimmers who need help more quickly than lifeguards who are stationed on the shore.

In addition to a rescue tube, first aid equipment, such as a first aid kit, may be carried in a boat. This lets the lifeguard begin first aid procedures immediately when needed.

figure 3-7 *A lifeguard stationed at deck level may either be stationary or roving.*

figure 3-6 *An elevated lifeguard station.*

Surveillance

Since they are responsible for the patrons in their area, lifeguards need good *scanning* techniques. Communication and cooperation with lifeguards in adjacent areas also help to ensure safety.

Lifeguards should continuously scan back and forth over the water slowly enough to be able to see what each patron is doing. Each sweep must cover the total area of responsibility. If a patron goes under water, the lifeguard must scan back to see that the swimmer surfaces. The lifeguard needs to carefully watch the water area directly in front of and below the lifeguard stand because it is a potential **blind spot.**

Zone coverage. Areas of responsibility are also called *zones.* Adjacent zones may overlap. No lifeguard should have a zone that requires a scan of more than 180 degrees.

Figure 3-9, *A* and *B* shows examples of overlapping zone coverage for stationary lifeguard stands. You can adapt them for your facility.

The following are some advantages of overlapping zone coverage:

* Lifeguards concentrate on a limited area.
* Overlapping zones allow double coverage.

figure 3-9 *Examples of zone coverage:* **A,** *two lifeguards;* **B,** *three lifeguards.*

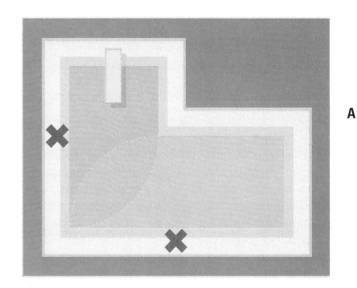

ZONE COVERAGE
2 LIFEGUARDS

A

figure 3-8 *A boat station at the outer edges of a swimming area.*

ZONE COVERAGE
3 LIFEGUARDS

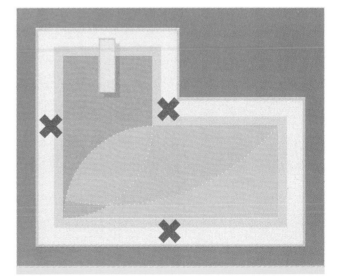

B

Disadvantages of overlapping zone coverage include the following:

- Large facilities have more zones and therefore need more staff.
- Lifeguards may be confused about their area of responsibility in areas where zones overlap.
- Lifeguards may not scan their entire zone if its boundaries are not clearly marked (lifelines, ladders, diving boards).

You can try to minimize these disadvantages in these ways:

- Concentrating swimmers in a few sections so that large swimming areas can be supervised more easily
- Ensuring that lifeguards are aware of their area of responsibility
- Establishing an effective system of communications among lifeguards

Total coverage. Another procedure for supervising patrons is for one lifeguard to be responsible for the entire swimming area (Fig. 3-10). Use this method only if a small number of patrons are in the water and only when

---

figure 3-10 *An example of total coverage.*

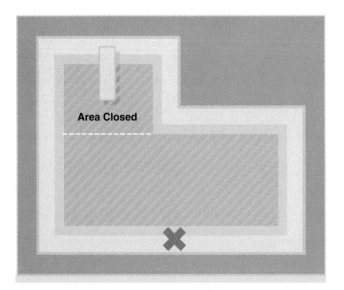

two lifeguards are on duty—one on surveillance duty and the other completing assigned tasks. An advantage of this system is that it requires a smaller number of staff. However, this system has the following disadvantages:

- The lifeguard is required to observe a larger area and may not see a problem as quickly as with zone coverage.
- The lifeguard may concentrate too much of his or her attention on the extreme boundaries of the area. He or she must be fully aware of all activity by continually scanning the entire area.

Try to minimize these disadvantages in these ways:

- Concentrate the patrons in a smaller area.
- Close some sections of the water area.

Backup coverage. In emergency situations when there are two or more lifeguards on duty and one lifeguard must enter the water, lifeguards who remain out of the water must supervise a larger area. They may need to move to better vantage points, depending on the facility's design. Figure 3-11, *A* illustrates zone coverage when three lifeguards are on surveillance duty. Figure 3-11, *B* shows an example of backup coverage for the same three-lifeguard facility. In Figure 3-11, *B* lifeguard Y is the primary rescuer. He or she signals and enters the water (indicated by a dotted line). The other two lifeguards (lifeguards X and Z) each stand in the lifeguard chairs and divide the responsibility for scanning the pool. (For further examples of backup coverage, see Chapter 7 in American Red Cross *Lifeguarding Today.*)

Rotation

The system used for ***rotation*** of lifeguards during their shifts should be clear and carried out professionally and safely at all times—even if only a few patrons are in the pool. Rotation of lifeguards helps maintain staff alertness. Lifeguards who move to new surveillance points at set times are less likely to become bored and lax in their surveillance.

When lifeguards are rotating from stand to stand, from stand to off surveillance, or from stand to some other duty, they must move in as timely, efficient, and safe a manner as possible. Rotating lifeguards must maintain constant surveillance of the zone of responsi-

figure 3-11 *A, Zone coverage for a three-lifeguard facility; and **B,** an example of backup coverage for the same three-life-guard facility.*

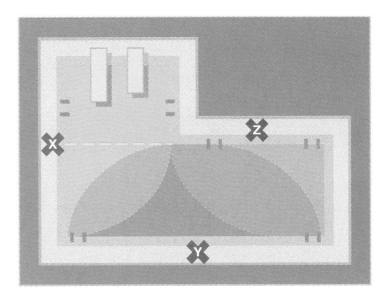

A

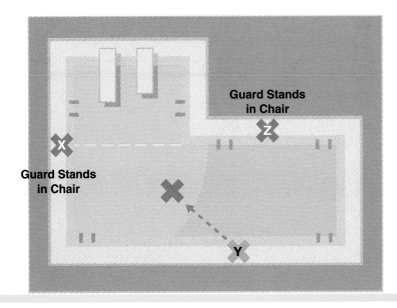

B

figure 3-12 *During a lifeguard rotation:* **A,** *the incoming lifeguard assumes a scanning position;* **B,** *the lifeguard who is being relieved passes the rescue equipment to the incoming lifeguard and prepares to come down off the stand and assume a scanning position;* **C,** *the rotation is complete when the incoming lifeguard is in position and is scanning the pool.*

A

B

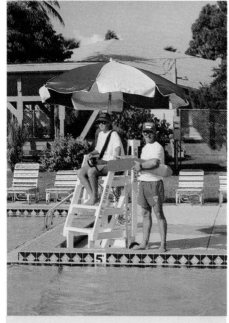

bility. The incoming lifeguard assumes a position that allows him or her to scan the area while the outgoing lifeguard comes down off the stand (Fig. 3-12, A). The lifeguard who is being relieved assumes a position to scan the zone or area while the incoming lifeguard gets on the stand or into the appropriate position (Fig. 3-12, B). The rotation is complete when the incoming lifeguard is in position, has the rescue tube in place, and is scanning the pool (Fig. 3-12, C).

Rotations should take place on a regular schedule. For example, a 30-minute rotation schedule allows a lifeguard to become acquainted with the zone yet does not allow him or her to become too comfortable or bored. Each lifeguard should be in a position long enough to become familiar with the hazards, crowd, weather, and other conditions from that **vantage point.**

Lifeguards should not be on the stand for more than 1 hour without a break. A typical schedule has a lifeguard guard for 1 hour and then break for 10 minutes. Remember that incidents can occur at any time—including during rotations and breaks. Rotations should follow a clockwise or counter-clockwise direction so that all areas of the facility are covered. Do not rotate all lifeguard stations simultaneously, since this can lead to breaks in the scanning of the pool or water area. Rotations should be easy to understand and follow (Fig. 3-13).

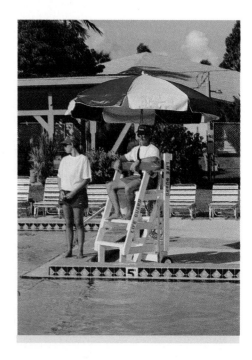

C

figure 3-13 *An example of a lifeguard rotation.*

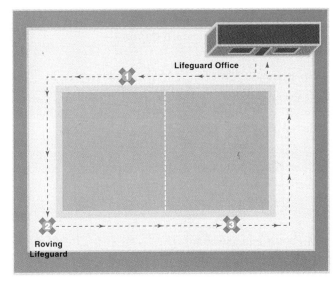

1. Lifeguard in the Office goes to Station 1
2. Lifeguard in Station 1 goes to Station 2
3. Lifeguard in Station 2 goes to Station 3
4. Lifeguard in Station 3 goes to Lifeguard Office
Rotation schedule every 20 minutes beginning at the start of the shift.

figure 3-14 *Facilities can manage various activities at the same time by dividing the facility into sections.*

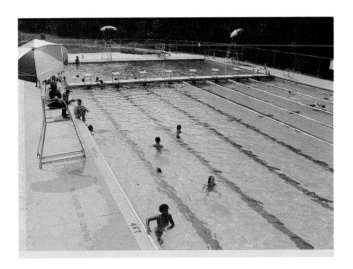

Programming

The programming at your facility affects not only the number of lifeguards on duty but also the training and preparation they receive. It also affects how you develop emergency action plans and the methods you choose for guarding the facility.

Facility management can manage various activities at the same time by dividing the swimming area into sections for various activities, such as (Fig. 3-14)—

- Recreational swimming.
- Swimming laps for physical conditioning.
- Diving.
- Instruction in swimming, snorkeling, and so on.

All sections require a lifeguard on duty. Open-water facilities may also have sections for boating or fishing. Be sure dangerous sections of tree stumps, rocks, large areas of weeds, or shallow water are posted "Danger— No Swimming," "Danger—No Boating," "Danger—No Diving," or "Danger—Shallow Water."

Types of programs. Common kinds of programs include instructional programs, competitive programs, recreational programs, fitness programs, and service and self-development programs. Following are examples of activities in each type along with implications for lifeguarding and facility preparation:

Instructional programs. (Age of participants—6 months and up)

Instructional programs include—

- Infant and preschool swimming.
- Learn-to-swim programs.
- Adult swimming lessons.
- Lifeguard training.
- Water safety instructor course.
- Skin diving.
- SCUBA diving.
- Kayaking or canoeing.

Each activity has specific hazards and safety concerns. If your facility does not have a list of precautions associated with each activity, develop one with your facility manager. Discuss these precautions with your lifeguards before the first meeting of a new class, and review them periodically.

When developing a list of precautions, consider these factors:

- *The activity.* Is the activity simple, such as swim lessons, or does it require more preparation, such as lifeguard training? By analyzing the activity, you also identify any risks associated with it.
- *Participant characteristics.* The age, skill, and fitness levels of the participants help you determine whether additional assistance or extra precautions are needed to avoid or control injuries or incidents.
- *Equipment used.* Participants may use a variety of equipment, such as flotation devices, training aids, and toys.

These factors help you develop a list of precautions for a specific activity. Following, for example, are precautions associated with infant and preschool lessons (Fig. 3-15):

Before class begins, lifeguards should—

- Review symptoms of hypothermia.
- Review skills for choking, rescue breathing, and CPR.
- Review policies for extracting human waste from the pool.
- Inspect any toys to be used in class for sharp edges, and dispose of broken toys.

- Make sure all training aids are in good condition.
- Check electrical outlets for safety plugs.
- Make sure infants and toddlers are wearing plastic pants or training pants that fit snugly around the legs and waist. Do not allow diapers in the pool.

During class, the lifeguard should—

- Be especially alert for children running on deck.
- Make sure infants and children are accompanied by a parent or other adult while in the water, if parents are included in the program.

Competitive programs. (Age of participants—6 years and up)

Competitive programs include (Fig. 3-16)—

- High school swimming.
- United States Swimming (Age group swimming).
- United States Diving.
- Masters Swimming.
- Recreational swim team programs.
- Water polo.
- **Synchronized swimming.**
- Lifeguard competitions.

figure 3-16 *Competitive swimming is one example of a competitive aquatic program.*

figure 3-15 *A list of precautions should be developed for aquatic activities, such as infant and preschool swim lessons.*

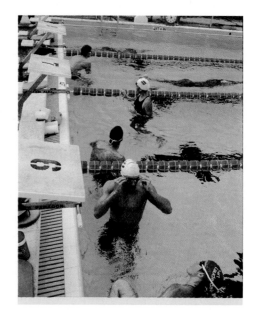

You and your lifeguards should know the safety policies set forth by the governing body of the competitive program. For example, lanes may be designated as sprint, start, or warm-up lanes during a warm-up period before competition. The lifeguard must ensure that swimmers follow the procedures set for lane activity.

A large number of swimmers may be in the water during practice sessions. You should determine the number of lifeguards on duty, based on the staffing policies established for the facility. Because of the large number of swimmers, scanning the bottom of the pool is extremely difficult during practice sessions. The lifeguard must carefully scan the surface at all times. Any time a swimmer submerges, the lifeguard should scan back to be sure he or she surfaces.

Supervision on the deck may also be different. In a swim meet, for example, with many people on the deck, including officials, coaches, swimmers, parents, photographers, television crews, and broadcasters, surveillance of people on the deck may be difficult. In such cases, you need to schedule enough lifeguards to ensure effective surveillance of both the deck and the water.

With competitive programs, consider also the surveillance and safety factors associated with competitive equipment and facility structures. Equipment such as lane lines and structures such as bulkheads can limit a lifeguard's effectiveness when performing a rescue or engaging in patron surveillance.

Recreational programs. (Age of participants—6 months and up)

Recreational programs include—

- Family swim.
- Open swimming.
- Dive-in movies.
- Water basketball.
- Water volleyball.
- Innertube water polo.
- Games night.

The most common recreational activity is the open swim (Fig. 3-17). During open swim, a facility may designate separate parts of the pool for recreational swimming, lap swimming, diving, and water basketball. Several activities can occur simultaneously.

During these activities, your lifeguards should be in positions with the best vantage for scanning and regulating activities. With certain activities, you must make special plans, preparations, and precautions. For example, "Dive-In Movies" have gained popularity in many aquatic facilities. Since a movie is being shown on a wall or screen in the pool area, lighting is an issue. Most state codes regulate lighting requirements. Your state may not allow this activity if proper lighting is not provided.

Fitness programs. (Age of participants—12 years and up)

Exercise and fitness activities are popular. Fitness programs include (Fig. 3-18)—

- Water aerobics.
- Water walking.
- Deep-water running.
- Lap swimming.
- Prenatal water fitness.

figure 3-17 *The most common recreational activity is open swim.*

figure 3-18 *Water exercise is a popular fitness program.*

Any **cardiovascular** exercise program has some risk factors. Because of the risk of someone becoming fatigued, your lifeguards should review first aid for heat cramps, heat exhaustion, heat stroke, and sudden illness.

Service and self-development programs. (Age of participants—6 months and up)

This type of program involves therapy and rehabilitation (Fig. 3-19). Service and self-development programs include—

- Arthritis classes.
- Disabled therapy.
- Physical therapy.
- Rehabilitation.
- Lessons for the developmentally delayed.

Your lifeguards should be familiar with the general conditions and abilities of participants in service and self-development programs. Review with your lifeguards the characteristics of these conditions and any care that made be needed. The following, for example, can be included in training for guarding a cardiac rehabilitation program:

- Review of facility emergency action plan, including contacting EMS personnel
- Review of signs and symptoms of a heart attack
- Review of care for a heart attack
- Oxygen administration (if applicable)

Special-use pools and structures

Many aquatic facilities have special-use pools and structures, such as *therapy pools,* competitive swimming and water polo pools, diving pools, wading pools, water slides, and spas. Effective safety policies and procedures, in-service training, and periodic review of policies and procedures related to special-use pools and structures promote a safe environment for these participants. As the head lifeguard, you and management should consider the risk factors of special-use pools and work to manage them. Provide specialized in-service training for your lifeguards for each special-use pool. Some of these safety factors are described in the following sections.

Pools

Lane lines. Lane lines can be an obstacle to lifeguards performing a rescue (Fig. 3-20). Train lifeguards how to perform rescues with lane lines in place. If they must be taken out to remove a victim from the water, your lifeguards should know how to remove them and where the lane line wrench is kept.

Bulkheads. Bulkheads in 50-meter pools can be a safety problem (Fig. 3-21). Most bulkheads are hollow. This invites patrons to swim directly beneath and surface inside the structure. A clear view of a patron beneath a bulkhead is impossible. Facility rules should prohibit swimming under a bulkhead. Another problem is that surveillance of both sides of the bulkhead is im-

---

figure 3-19 *Service and self-development programs involve therapy and rehabilitation.*

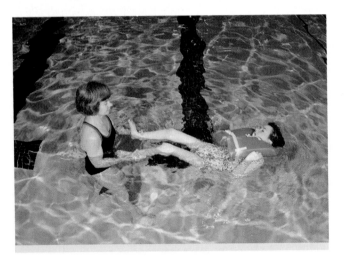

---

figure 3-20 *Lane lines can be obstacles to lifeguards performing a rescue.*

possible unless the lifeguard is standing directly to the side of it. Lifeguards must be located to allow surveillance of the entire bottom. At least two lifeguards are necessary in pools with bulkheads if swimming is allowed in both sections.

Do not allow patrons to walk on or dive from a bulkhead. Often bulkheads are quite high above the surface of the water, and generally there is shallow water to one side, making diving unsafe.

Deep pools. Some pools are constructed with no shallow water area. Deep pools often allow faster swimming because of less water turbulence. Lifeguards must practice procedures for spinal injury management with lane lines in place and in deep water. You may want to store swim fins at the lifeguard stands, since fins make it easier to retrieve a victim from the pool bottom and maintain effective in-line stabilization at the surface.

Competitive water polo. The sport of water polo may involve special facility and equipment characteristics. Water polo events are usually in deep pools, with rescue implications for suspected spinal injuries or unconscious victims. Although the likelihood of a spinal injury occurring in deep water is remote, you should still have an emergency action plan for rescuing and removing a victim from the water.

Boundary lines may create a major problem for handling spinal injuries or rescuing an unconscious victim. Teach lifeguards how to remove the lines to remove the victim from the water.

Common injuries players may suffer include scrapes, cramps, cuts, bruises, swelling, bloody or broken noses,

eye injuries, or injuries to toes, fingers, or hands. Have your lifeguards review and be prepared to give first aid for these injuries. A resuscitation mask, disposable latex gloves, and eye protectors should be at hand.

Diving pools. Diving pools are generally deeper than other pools, ranging from 14 feet to 20 feet deep. The diving facility may have 1- and 3-meter diving boards, as well as 1-, 3-, 5-, 7½-, and 10-meter platforms (Fig. 3-22).

A variety of injuries can occur at diving facilities. Most injuries result from lack of supervision. Injuries include **abrasions, lacerations,** bruises, swelling, broken bones, **concussions,** fractured skulls, broken eardrums, and neck or back injuries. Injuries may be caused by striking the diving board or platform, falling from the ladder leading to the diving board onto the deck, landing flat onto the surface of the water, slipping and falling on the diving board or platform, and stumbling on the ladder to the board or platform.

Review with your lifeguards the signs and symptoms of these injuries, along with their care. Develop an emergency action plan for the diving facility, and practice it regularly.

Spinal injuries occur more often in unsupervised areas, such as pools in backyards, hotels/motels, and apartment complexes. Typically these victims enter the water headfirst, and as a result of insufficient distance in front of the board, they strike the upslope of the bottom of the pool. Though spinal injuries are extremely rare in deep pools, lifeguards still need to practice spinal

figure 3-21 *Bulkheads can be a safety and surveillance problem.*

figure 3-22 *A diving facility may have 1- and 3-meter diving boards.*

injury management for deep-water pools. Take the pool's individual characteristics into account when you develop emergency spinal injury management procedures.

You should consider restricting the use of diving platforms over 3 meters in height to competitive divers directly supervised by a qualified diving coach or instructor. Severe injuries may result when untrained divers jump or dive from a height of more than 3 meters.

In pools with a dark bottom, lifeguards have difficulty seeing people on the bottom, especially people with darker skin. Lifeguards should watch for each diver to return to the surface. Water agitation on the surface created by a diver entering the water also makes it difficult to see the pool bottom. Lifeguards should be positioned where they can best see the bottom. Do not allow other patrons in the diving pool during diving activities.

Problems With Deep Water Rescues

The depth of the pool creates two problems. The deeper a person descends, the greater the risk of rupturing an eardrum. Competitive divers generally equalize pressure in their ears during descent, but congestion from a cold or allergies may make it difficult for the diver to equalize pressure.

Your lifeguards need to know how to equalize the pressure in their ears to avoid rupturing an eardrum during deep-water rescue. Pinch the nostrils together and gently try to blow out through the nose to equalize pressure while descending.

The second problem relates to buoyancy. As a person descends, the water pressure increases. The deeper one descends, the greater the pressure. During descent, the lungs are compressed, causing decreased buoyancy. If the victim is on the bottom in deep water, it is more difficult to bring him or her to the surface because both the rescuer and victim have lost buoyancy as a result of pressure on the lungs.

The rescuer needs a strong kick to bring a victim to the surface in deep water (14 to 20 feet in depth).

Before diving competitions, you or your supervisor should notify coaches of the facility's policies and procedures. Post signs near the diving boards or platforms that specify rules, regulations, and procedures (Fig. 3-23). This helps maintain consistency and safety for all coaches and diving teams using the facility.

Include all diving policies in your in-service training program. Brief lifeguards on what types of injuries occur, diving rules and regulations, their responsibility for safety, and rescue procedures.

Wading pools. Wading pools generally range from a depth of $\frac{1}{2}$ foot to 3 feet (Fig. 3-24). Post specific rules to regulate the following:

- The maximum age limit for use of the pool
- What toys, if any, may be used in the pool
- If a parent or adult needs to supervise a child and where he or she should be located, such as the edge of the pool or within 5 feet of the edge of the pool
- What activities are unacceptable
- What swimwear is required for young children, such as plastic pants for children wearing diapers

---

figure 3-23 *A sign displaying diving rules and regulations should be posted near the diving boards.*

Because of the age and swimming abilities of the swimmers in the wading pool, take extra measures to ensure their safety. Assign a lifeguard to monitor the wading pool.

Water slides. Many new facilities are built with slides, and many older facilities are adding them (Fig. 3-25). Slides add a dimension to the facility that deserves special attention. Slides vary widely in size and shape. Policies that apply to all slides to reduce the risk of injury include—

- Locating the slide in deep water.
- Requiring patrons to slide feetfirst.
- Locating a lifeguard at the top of the slide or at the steps to control slide use.
- Allowing only one patron at a time to slide.
- Making sure the patron in the **catch pool** swims directly to the pool edge before allowing the next person to slide.
- Requiring a swimming test before participants are allowed to use the slide.
- Ensuring that water is continually running down the slide.
- Securing buoys and lines in the catch pool to mark boundaries and keep swimmers out of the area.
- Not allowing swimming in the catch pool.

Give specific in-service training for guarding water slides. This training should address characteristics of the facility, rules and regulations, emergency action plans, common injuries, and first aid for common injuries. The American Red Cross Waterpark Lifeguarding module provides information on water slides and other structures. This module can be taught as part of the in-service training.

Play structures. As patrons seek more variety at aquatic facilities, play structures are becoming increasingly common. Permanent play structures include sprays, fountains, and climb-on animals (Fig. 3-26). Non-permanent entertainment features include large floating toys, inflatable play structures, and in-water basketball and volleyball (Fig. 3-27). At some newer pools, entertainment features are part of the pool's design from the beginning. At older pools, permanent play structures are being added—sometimes replacing other equipment like diving boards. At many facilities, removable play structures permit different activities to take place during the day.

Because of their different shapes and sizes, play structures pose a unique surveillance challenge for lifeguards. Depending on the particular structure's features, many blind spots may exist, making it hard for a single lifeguard to provide effective surveillance. You may

figure 3-24 *A lifeguard should be assigned to monitor a wading pool.*

figure 3-25 *Water slides are an added attraction.*

figure 3-26 *Permanent play structures include sprays and fountains.*

figure 3-27 *Non-permanent entertainment features include inflatable play structures.*

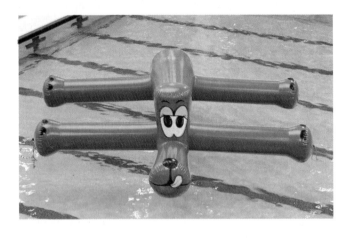

figure 3-28 *Many aquatic facilities have spas.*

have to add lifeguarding staff to effectively cover a play structure. In some cases, you may use lifeguards who monitor only a specific play structure and nothing else, especially when many patrons are using it. Position your lifeguards so that they have a clear view of all parts of the play structure and the surrounding area. Depending on the structure's features and number of patrons using it, you may have to position a lifeguard in the water for additional safety.

Your lifeguards must take precautions beyond the basic principles of patron surveillance when guarding a play structure. Teach your lifeguards about these precautions by briefing them on the following general points:

- *The excitement of these features may encourage non-swimmers or weak swimmers to be careless.* They might try things they might not ordinarily do, or they might enter deep water without intending to do so.
- *Sprays and fountains are usually in shallow water.* Children who are excited may run and fall and injure themselves. A very young child who falls might not be able to get back up.
- *Moving water may surprise patrons.* They might lose their balance and be unable to stand up again.
- *Patrons may climb onto floating toys and jump back into the water.* They are likely not to notice what is around them and thus jump onto other patrons. Do not let patrons dive from these floating toys. They can injure themselves, especially if the structure is in shallow water.
- *Do not let a play structure become overcrowded.* Be prepared to restrict the number of patrons who use it at any given time. It may be useful, for instance, to form groups to use the structure or to have a waiting line. Or you may segregate users by age for safety.

Additional precautions may be needed for certain play structures, such as an inflatable water slide. Consult with your facility manager, and review the safety guidelines provided by the manufacturer. Brief your lifeguards on these additional precautions.

Spas. Many swimming facilities have *spas* (Fig. 3-28). Spas can be a relaxing and enjoyable addition to the facility if they are maintained and regulated properly. Drownings in spas often result from the patron drinking alcohol, having a reaction to hot water, entangling hair in bottom drains, or falling unconscious into the spa after striking the head. As the head lifeguard, you must understand these risks and make sure your lifeguards do also. Review with your lifeguards the facility's rules for spas, such as the following:

- Shower with warm water and soap before entering the spa.
- Enter and exit the spa slowly and cautiously.
- The following people should not use the spa:
  - Those with heart disease, diabetes, high or low blood pressure, circulatory problems, stress problems, seizures, and epilepsy.
  - Those who are on diets or are using prescribed or recreational drugs.
- Pregnant women can use the spa for up to 15 minutes if the temperature is below 102 degrees F.
- Unsupervised children may not use the spa.
- Children under 5 years of age are not allowed to use the spa because they are not physically capable of coping with the heat.
- Do not use the spa while under the influence of alcohol or drugs.
- Do not use the spa alone.
- No diving or jumping into the spa.
- Do not stay in the spa for more than 15 minutes; you may shower, cool down, drink some water, and if you wish, return for another brief stay. Long exposure may result in nausea, dizziness, or fainting.
- Do not use body lotions, oils, or suntan preparations before going in the spa.
- Do not wear street shoes in the spa.
- No food or drink is allowed in the spa.
- Do not submerge to the bottom of the spa. Hair may become entangled in the drain.
- Do not exercise aerobically in the spa. Stretching exercises are permitted.

Therapy pools. A therapy pool generally has easy access through graduated steps, a gentle sloping ramp, or lifts. This pool is designed for physical therapy, often involving guidance and supervision by a physician or a physical therapist. The temperature of a therapy pool generally ranges from 85 degrees F to 95 degrees F, and the water may be agitated by jets. This type of pool is typically used for rehabilitation by the elderly, accident victims, stroke victims, individuals with physical disabilities, and very young children (infant, toddler, and preschool classes). You and your lifeguards need to be aware of risks that accompany this type of pool. Warmer water temperatures, for example, may increase the probability of heat cramps and heat exhaustion.

FACILITY SURVEILLANCE

As the head lifeguard, you are responsible for the health and safety of your lifeguarding staff and facility patrons. Providing a safe and well-kept facility is part of this responsibility.

The health, sanitation, and security procedures of an aquatic facility are set by facility management, based on local or state health department regulations and equipment manufacturers' directions for care. Your facility's policies and procedures manual should include, at a minimum, the following information about health, sanitation, and security of the facility:

- A safety checklist of items to be inspected, by you and your lifeguards, on a daily, weekly, or monthly schedule.
- An outline of procedures to be followed for maintenance or repairs of broken fixtures or equipment.
- The areas of the facility to be cleaned on a daily, weekly, or monthly schedule, the cleaning procedures to be followed, and who is responsible for the cleaning (your lifeguards or maintenance personnel).
- A checklist of items to be inspected by you and your lifeguards immediately after the facility is closed and procedures for securing the building for the night. Security procedures are best conducted by two lifeguards, one witnessing the steps the other takes.

Safety inspections

Ensure that all equipment in the facility, recreational and rescue equipment, is inspected daily. (See Appendix D.) Any unsatisfactory area or piece of equipment that cannot be immediately corrected by you or your lifeguards must be closed or removed until it can be repaired or replaced (Fig. 3-29). Ensure that your lifeguards notify you immediately if they identify a hazard. Follow the facility procedures for this situation. This may be as simple as notifying your supervisor, who will complete a work order to have the situation corrected.

When performing a safety check, inspect all areas open to patrons, including locker rooms, showers, toilets, and deck areas, where patrons enter the facility.

Common problem areas and identifiable hazards in aquatic facilities follow.

figure 3-29 *A diving board closed for repairs.*

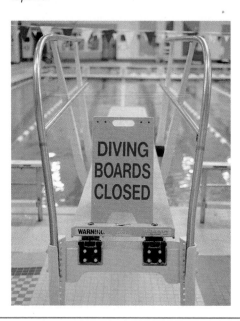

figure 3-30 *A, Leaky shower heads and B, sharp edges on lockers are some of the items that should be checked in locker rooms and showers.*

A

B

Locker rooms and showers. Inspect locker rooms and showers for the following (Fig. 3-30, *A* and *B*):

- Standing pools of water and slippery surfaces
- Leaky faucets, shower heads, and toilets
- Broken chairs and benches, broken or missing clothes hooks
- Stopped-up floor drains
- Broken or leaky pipes and spigots
- Temperature of the shower water, too hot or too cold
- Broken floor tiles
- Broken lights, hand dryers, or electrical fixtures
- Sharp edges on lockers
- Equipment in place
  - Emergency lighting
  - Fire extinguishers
  - Trash receptacles

Pool area. Inspect the pool area for the following (Fig. 3-31, *A-D*):

Decks and entrance areas

- Slippery surfaces
- Broken or loose concrete
- Coping tiles, check for loose concrete

Overflow troughs

- Broken, chipped, or loose tiles
- Debris

Ladders

- Loose or broken steps
- Splinters (wooden ladders)
- Sharp edges, exposed nails or bolts
- Loose or broken hand rails

Diving boards

- Slippery board surfaces created by algae, dust, body oils, or suntan lotions
- Nonskid surface worn
- Diving boards in poor condition; warped, obvious stress fractures, loose rivets

figure 3-31 *Some items to inspect around the pool area include—**A**, entrance areas;* ***B**, overflow troughs;* ***C**, movable fulcrum;* and ***D**, lifeguard chairs.*

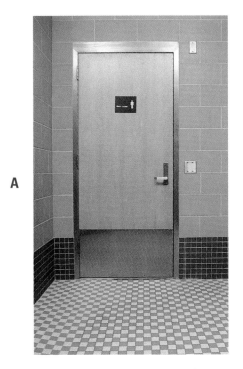

A

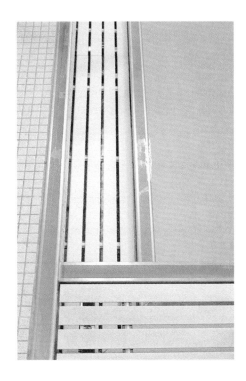

B

C

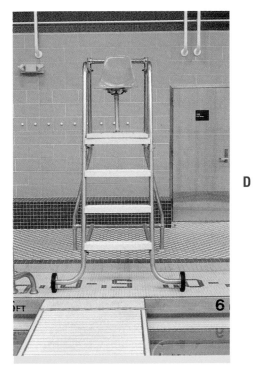

D

Diving stand

- Board is loose or not bolted to stand
- Fulcrum padding not in place
- Loose, broken, or misaligned fulcrum (loose bolts, rivets, or welds that attach stationary fulcrums to the stand or the wheel on movable fulcrums is not secured to the fulcrum)
- Loose or broken steps
- Loose or broken frame and railings
- Sharp edges, exposed nails or bolts
- Loose bolts

Diving platforms (towers)

- Nonskid surface worn
- Loose railings
- Loose or broken steps to the platform

Starting blocks (platforms)

- Starting blocks not located in deep water
- Nonskid surface area worn
- Base not secured to the deck
- Sharp edges, rust formation, and loose fittings
- Backstroke grips loose; inspect for sharp surfaces

Disabled lifts

- Base of lift loose or not secured to the deck
- Movable parts not operating properly
- Loose hinges, bolts, and welds
- Sharp edges on parts of the lift
- Lift unable to support weight-bearing operation

Disabled ramps

- Nonskid surface worn
- Hand rails loose or unstable; loose fittings at anchor points
- Sharp edges and rust on rails

Lifeguard stands (stationary and portable)

- Loose or broken steps
- Loose or broken frame or wheels
- Sharp edges, exposed nails or bolts
- Loose bolts and rivets; fractured welds
- Broken brackets that secure umbrellas
- Stand unstable or not firmly anchored

Spas and wading pools. Be sure inspections are conducted during the day to determine pool clarity, chemical levels, and water temperature. Carefully inspect the following in spas and wading pools (Fig. 3-32, *A* and *B*):

Drain covers

- Cover not centered over the drain
- Cover not secured to the bottom
- Cracks or sharp edges

Tiles and plaster

- Chipped or broken tiles
- Rough or sharp edges in the plaster

Steps and railings

- Steps not clearly marked on the top and side edges
- Nonskid surfaces on steps are worn
- Loose or broken hand railings

Concrete

- Chipping and sharp edges around areas of the wading pool

Waterfront facilities. Waterfront facilities often have unique areas and structures. Inspection procedures should include checking these. Along with checking the water depths at waterfronts, check for the following (Fig. 3-33):

Beach area

- Glass or sharp objects
- Holes
- Rocks

Docks

- Floats
- Exposed nails
- Broken or splintered boards
- Broken or loose boards or decking
- Unstable lifeguard platforms

figure 3-32 *A* and *B*, *The drain covers, steps, and railings should be inspected in both wading pools and spas.*

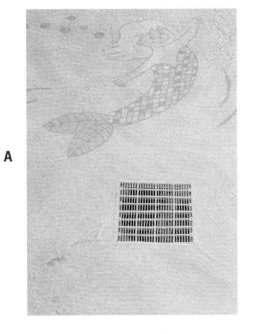

A

B

figure 3-33 *Waterfront beach areas should be checked for safety.*

Other structures. Some facilities have other unique areas and structures. Inspection procedures should include these areas and structures, as well as the following (Fig. 3-34, *A* and *B*):

Water slides

- Obstructions in the slide path
- Surface cracks
- Rough patchwork at slide joints
- Leaking joint seals
- Loose risers on the turns
- Excessive movement of the flume
- Insufficient water flow in the slide
- Incorrect water level within the catch pool

figure 3-34 *A and B, Water slides and play structures should be inspected for stability and surface cracks.*

Play structures

- Permanent play structure unstable or not firmly anchored
- Broken, loose, or inoperable moving parts
- Cracked plastic
- Cracks or holes in inflatable play structures
- Inflatable play structure not firmly anchored
- Water not properly spouting from water fountains

First aid stations. Inspect the first aid station daily for unclean conditions, insufficient supplies, and damaged or outdated inventory (Fig. 3-35). The first aid station should also be inspected to ensure it has the following items:

- First aid procedures posted and in clear view
- Pens, pencils, and paper
- Incident Report forms with sample guide
- Liquid antibacterial soap
- Cot, blankets, and pillow
- Flashlight
- Plastic bags of various sizes
- Paper towels and cups
- Trash container
- Emergency phone numbers and procedures
- Portable first aid kit
- Adhesive compresses of various sizes (adhesive strips)
- Adhesive tape
- Eye dressing pads

figure 3-35 *First aid stations should be inspected daily.*

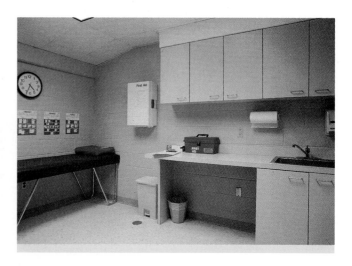

- Gauze pads
- Roller gauze
- Scissors and tweezers
- Triangular bandages
- Cold packs
- Disposable latex gloves
- Hazardous waste containers
- Pocket masks
- Bag valve masks
- *American Red Cross CPR for the Professional Rescuer* participant's manual
- *American Red Cross Lifeguarding Today* participant's manual
- Resuscitator and oxygen (special training required)
- Splints
- Long backboard with at least three straps and a commercial head immobilizer

Other important items and areas to inspect. Rescue equipment and maintenance equipment, such as rescue tubes and pool vacuums, should be inspected to make sure that they are in good working condition.

The bottom and sides of the pool are other areas to check. Since the water in swimming pools is normally clear, lifeguards can visually inspect the pool by walking around it and looking for hazards, such as underwater lights that have worked loose or have broken glass.

At waterfronts, lifeguards can check the bottom by carefully walking through the shallow water and by swimming through the deeper areas with a mask and fins.

Facility maintenance

All personnel at aquatic facilities work together to provide programs in recreation, competition, education, and safety. All patrons participating in these programs expect the facility to be attractive, comfortable, clean, and healthful. You can meet the patrons' expectations by ensuring that you and your lifeguards maintain a well-kept facility. You can do this by following a daily maintenance routine that includes cleaning all areas of the facility.

The following is a daily maintenance routine you can adapt to your facility:

Before opening the facility

- Check the bottom of the swimming area for hazardous objects, and check sand bottom swimming

areas for build up of ridges that may cause diving injuries.
- Sweep out and hose down locker rooms, bathhouses, showers, toilets, and entrance ways. These areas should be scrubbed and disinfected daily.
- Skim the surface of the water, and remove debris from overflow troughs in swimming pools.
- Brush and vacuum the pool sides and bottom.
- Rake the beach at waterfronts. Inspect the area for debris.
- Empty all trash containers daily. Clean and disinfect the containers weekly.
- Clean the office, lifeguard room, and first aid room. Wash treatment surfaces in the first aid room with a disinfectant.
- Check lifelines to see that they are properly located, stretched tightly enough to support an adult with his or her head above water, and anchored properly.
- Hose down the deck or dock area. At waterfronts, you can do this with buckets of water. Wash in a direction away from the swimming area, if possible, to avoid splashing or washing any debris from the deck into the pool.

During hours of operation (periodically)

- Remove all trash.
- Replenish any needed supplies.
- Inspect the pool deck or beach area.
- Inspect the areas used for sunbathing.
- Inspect locker rooms and floor.
- Inspect toilets and showers.
- Disinfect bench surfaces.

At closing

- Check the bottom of the swimming area for objects.
- Put trash in cans and station them where they can be picked up.
- Disinfect and hose down the locker rooms, and shut off the showers and faucets.
- Hose down the pool deck or dock area.
- Put all lost-and-found articles in a designated area.
- Return all equipment to the proper area.
- Turn off all unnecessary lights. Turn on any security lighting.
- Check all windows, doors, and gates to be sure they are locked. (This should be done with another life-

guard or staff member who witnesses the security procedure.)

- Be sure all rented or borrowed equipment has been returned.

Pool water

To provide a safe swimming environment for your patrons, the clarity and quality of the pool water must be checked periodically. If water is clear, you should be able to clearly view the pool bottom and easily recognize racing lanes and drain covers (Fig. 3-36). If not, notify your supervisor so that corrective actions can be taken—the facility may have to be closed until the situation is corrected.

As head lifeguard, the monitoring and maintaining of the water clarity and quality may or may not be your duty. If maintaining water clarity and quality is your job, you or your supervisor should ensure that you have the appropriate training in pool chemistry and operation, such as by taking a pool operator program offered by state or local governments and national organizations. (Refer to Appendix C for a listing of organizations that offer pool operator programs.)

Water quality is determined by testing chemicals and minerals in the water. How often the water is tested and the tests used vary according to state and local ordinances. In general, chemical levels are checked at least four times a day: at opening, mid morning, mid after-

noon, and closing. Outdoor pools may require more frequent checks due to environmental factors, such as rain and exposure to the sun. Testing should follow the manufacturers' directions included with the test kit (Fig. 3-37). In pools using electronic monitoring devices, the water should be checked manually at least once a day. Always refer to local or state ordinances for specific requirements.

Chemical handling and safety

Many chemicals are found in and around pools. Most important, ensure that all chemicals and cleaning agents are stored in their original containers and in the correct location. This site should not be left unattended or be accessible to anyone not trained to use these chemicals. Your employer should provide training and specific information about chemicals with which you are involved. This training should include **Material Safety Data Sheets (MSDS)**, proper storage and handling procedures, and emergency procedures for chemical spills of all kinds. Where required, a **self-contained breathing apparatus** should be stored outside and away from the chemical storage area.

Electrical safety

Electrical shock is a risk in the operation of swimming pools. Permanent and temporary electrical connections

figure 3-36 *If the pool water is sufficiently clear, you should be able to see the main drain cover from the deck.*

figure 3-37 *Follow the manufacturers' instructions when using a test kit to check the water quality of a pool.*

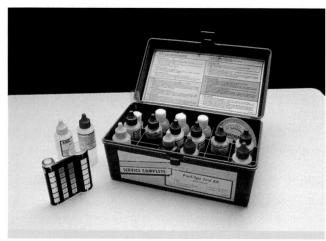

and wires for the following equipment may come in contact with water:

- Underwater lighting
- Stereo systems
- Automatic timing devices
- Pace clocks
- Electronic speakers
- Start systems
- Pool vacuum cleaners

All electrical devices should be connected to the power supply only from a **ground fault interrupter (GFI)** (Fig. 3-38). State and local electrical codes are very strict about positioning of electrical outlets and the use of electrical devices around pools. Rooms and boxes containing electrical equipment should stay locked. Only authorized personnel should be allowed in those areas.

figure 3-38 *An electrical outlet with a ground fault interrupter (GFI).*

INCIDENT AND INJURY CHART

Another means to support your efforts at injury prevention is an incident and injury chart. This is a diagram used to record injuries at your facility (Table 3-1). Such a chart depicts where and how injuries have happened, as well as the type of injury. This information can help you to eliminate or minimize any dangerous or potentially dangerous conditions.

An incident and injury chart usually shows all pieces of equipment, such as lifeguard stands, lifelines, ladders, and diving boards. Fences and deck and grass areas also are shown. Whenever there is an incident or injury, it is assigned a code and posted on the chart. By keeping track of all incidents and injuries, their frequency, and locations, it may be possible to determine their causes and effects. Then you or your facility manager can devise an action plan, which might include performing necessary maintenance, installing safety equipment, placing extra lifeguards on duty, or reassigning lifeguards for better supervision.

FACILITY SECURITY

All facilities require some sort of security. Security involves the safety of patrons when the facility is open and protection for the facility when it is closed. Security measures may include alarm systems, video surveillance, barriers, and policies for locking the facility.

Alarm systems. There are many types of alarm systems, including water **sensors** (which sense water agitation and may turn lights on in the facility or sound an audible alarm), electronic eyes, and sensors built into the pool deck. These sensors can be activated at times when participants should not be in that part of the facility and lifeguards are not on duty and when the facility is closed to alert security personnel if people enter the pool or pool area (Fig. 3-39).

Video surveillance. Some facilities use video surveillance during the day or evening (Fig. 3-40). During the day, it helps identify who is in the facility and where they are. Video surveillance can determine if someone enters a part of the facility where he or she should not be.

table 3-1 *Incident Chart*

#	Date	Time	Location	Type of Incident	Cause	Injured Area	Bather Load	Lifeguards on Duty	Water Conditions	Comments
1	5/30/93	1:45 pm	Diving Well	Near Drowning	Poor Ability	N/A	150	2	Clear	_____
2	6/11/93	12:15 pm	6' Wall	Near Drowning	Misjudg. Depth	N/A	125	2	Clear	_____
3	6/18/93	10:30 am	Diving Well	Drowning	Unknown	N/A	75	1	Cloudy	_____
4	6/21/93	11:15 am	Men's Entrance	Fall	Slippery Deck	Right Elbow	25	1	N/A	_____
5	6/21/93	2:30 pm	Shall. End Deck	Fall	Running	Left Knee	175	2	N/A	_____
6	7/2/93	3:30 pm	3.5' Wall	Spinal Injury	Diving	Head & Neck	160	2	Clear	_____
7	7/2/93	7:00 pm	4' Area	Tired Swimmer	Exhaustion	N/A	15	1	Clear	_____
8	7/3/93	2:10 pm	Diving Well	Near Drowning	Poor Ability	N/A	190	2	Clear	_____
9	7/4/93	11:00 am	3.5' Wall	Distress. Swim.	Misjudg. Depth	N/A	100	1	Clear	_____
10	7/4/93	1:30 pm	Pump Room	Chemical Burn	Unlocked Door	Both Hands	135	2	N/A	_____
11	7/11/93	12:30 pm	Diving Well	Distress. Swim.	Poor Ability	N/A	125	2	Clear	_____
12	7/15/93	10:45 am	4' Wall	Spinal Injury	Diving	Head & Neck	15	1	Clear	_____
13	7/24/93	7:30 pm	3.5' Wall	Argument	Lap Swimming	N/A	30	1	Clear	_____
14	7/28/93	5:30 pm	Pool Center	Tired Swimmer	Exhaustion	N/A	90	1	Clear	_____
15	8/1/93	3:45 pm	Diving Well	Near Drowning	Poor Ability	N/A	160	2	Clear	_____
16	8/1/93	4:15 pm	Diving Well	Near Drowning	Poor Ability	N/A	160	2	Clear	_____
17	8/7/93	10:45 am	Men's Entrance	Fall	Slippery Deck	Left Arm	20	1	N/A	_____
18	8/7/93	11:15 am	Men's Entrance	Fall	Slippery Deck	Left Ankle	25	1	N/A	_____
19	8/15/93	11:45 am	Men's Entrance	Fight	Unknown	N/A	10	1	N/A	_____
20	8/30/93	10:45 am	3.5' Wall	Distress. Swim.	Misjudg. Depth	N/A	120	1	Clear	_____
21	9/2/93	11:45 am	Diving Well	Near Drowning	Poor Ability	N/A	110	1	Clear	_____
22	9/5/93	2:15 pm	3.5' Wall	Distress. Swim.	Misjudg. Depth	N/A	190	2	Clear	_____
23										_____
24										_____
25										_____

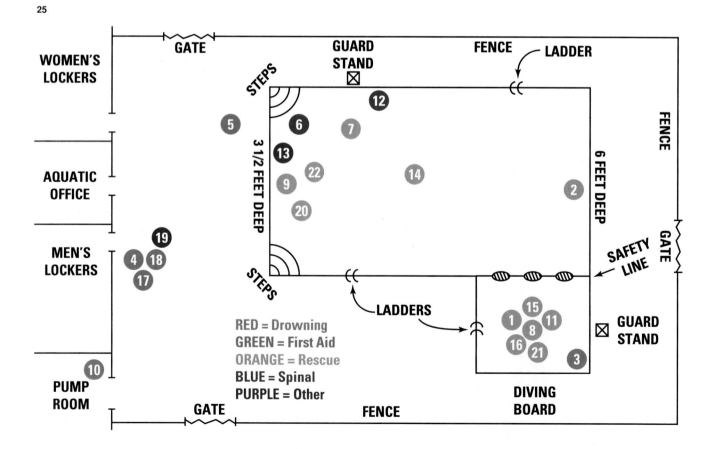

RED = Drowning
GREEN = First Aid
ORANGE = Rescue
BLUE = Spinal
PURPLE = Other

figure 3-39 *Alarm systems alert security personnel when someone enters a closed pool or pool area.*

figure 3-40 *Some facilities use video surveillance to help identify who is in the facility and where they are.*

Some pools have underwater cameras that scan the pool bottom. This system can also record acts of vandalism while the facility is open or closed.

Barriers. Barriers include gates, doors, fences, and walls (Fig. 3-41). The purpose of a barrier is to prevent people from entering a facility when and where they are not supposed to enter. Barriers must be inspected daily to ensure that they are operating properly. Check hinges, locks, and handles on gates and doors. Check to see that fences are sturdy and that no openings are present at the bottom of the fence or at sections where the fence is next to a building or wall. Check fences also for holes. Inspect walls for loose fittings and solid construction. Any malfunction or damage to barriers must be repaired immediately.

One of the most critical factors in facility security is access to the swimming area when no lifeguard or instructor is present. Access to the pool area should be restricted to times when a lifeguard is on duty.

The door from the locker room to the swimming area should be locked until a lifeguard opens it. For open recreational swimming, patrons should be kept out of the water until the lifeguard is on duty and at his or her station. Instructors should not allow class members into the water until the lifeguard signals readiness.

At the end of the day, have your lifeguards carefully scan the bleachers, deck, water, and pool bottom. Your lifeguards should also check restrooms and other areas. Once your lifeguards are certain no patrons remain, all doors should be locked and tested for security.

figure 3-41 *A barrier, such as a gate, prevents people from entering a facility when and where they are not supposed to enter.*

Vandalism protection

Vandalism protection involves procedures for closing a facility to protect it from vandalism while unoccupied. It can be very costly to repair damage caused by vandals.

The facility can take precautions to eliminate or decrease the occurrence of vandalism. You can help facility management assess the facility's procedures. The following are some precautions you and facility management can take:

• In indoor facilities, make sure the roof is sturdy and sound and that there are no obvious weak spots that will attract thieves or vandals. Any skylights should be secured each evening when the facility is closed. Close and lock any access from the roof to any part of the facility.
• Extra night lights at vulnerable spots around the building will double and sometimes triple protection. Thieves and vandals shy away from powerful lights.
• Be very certain to carefully check the facility's interior each night at closing time to be sure no one is hidden inside. This includes shower and toilet stalls, maintenance rooms, restrooms, below staircases, and behind counters. Check overflow troughs that are large enough to conceal an adult.
• Have a double-check system to make sure all windows and doors are securely locked every night.
• Ask the local police department to check the building thoroughly at least once a year. They may be able to make further recommendations to help protect the facility.
• Periodically check all walls of the building for deterioration or damage. Check all windows in the building from time to time for loose panes, weather-eroded sashes, insecure locks, and warped metal frames.

SUMMARY

Every aquatic facility can be a safe and inviting attraction if you and your lifeguard team take proper precautions to ensure a healthy environment. Policies and procedures for the three injury prevention strategies—communication, patron surveillance, and facility surveillance—help clarify the roles of facility management, you as head lifeguard, and your whole lifeguard team.

Since aquatic facilities have many features that could lead to injuries or other serious problems, all staff have responsibilities for proper operation and safety of the facility. You as head lifeguard play an integral part in providing this healthy environment.

STUDY QUESTIONS

Circle the letter of the best answer or answers.

1. Which of the following would be an acceptable explanation as to why a patron should not dive into shallow water.
   a) Not being injured in the past is no guarantee that one will not be injured now or in the future.
   b) Diving from the side of a pool into shallow water is a complex skill that requires training and experience.
   c) Dives into shallow water performed when one was a child are dangerous now because the person has become taller and dives with greater velocity.
   d) The rules say "No diving," and the rules must be followed.

2. Effective methods for developing lifeguard schedules include which of the following?
   a) Hire staff to fill designated shifts.
   b) Post shifts that need to be filled, and let staff sign up for them. Assign those shifts not filled.
   c) Assign shifts based on set criteria.
   d) Always give the newest hire the least desirable shift.
   e) Hire staff to work weekday hours, but assign the number of shifts or hours worked based on performance evaluations.

3. When determining where to locate lifeguard stations, take which of the following factors into consideration?
   a) Size and shape of the facility.
   b) Type of activity.
   c) Number of patrons in the facility.
   d) Depth of the water.
   e) Water clarity.

4. Which of the following precautions should be taken with infant and preschool swimming lessons?
   a) Make sure all training aids are in good condition.
   b) Check electrical outlets for safety plugs.
   c) Review policies for extracting human waste from the pool.
   d) Review first aid for heat cramps, heat exhaustion, heat stroke, and sudden illness.
   e) Review symptoms of hypothermia.
   f) Make sure infants and children are accompanied by an adult while in the water, if parents are involved in the program.
   g) Review care for a heart attack.

5. Which of the following policies apply to all water slides to reduce the risk of injury?
   a) Locate all slides in deep water.
   b) All patrons must slide feetfirst.
   c) No more than two patrons at a time can slide.
   d) Water must continually run down the slide.
   e) A lifeguard must be at the top of the slide or at the steps to control slide use.

6. Which of the following rules apply to spa safety?
   a) Enter and exit the spa slowly and cautiously.
   b) Pregnant women can use the spa for up to 15 minutes if the temperature is below 102 degrees F.
   c) People who are on diets should not use the spa.
   d) Do not use the spa while under the influence of alcohol or drugs.
   e) No diving or jumping into the spa.
   f) Do not submerge to the bottom of the spa.
   g) Do not do stretching exercises in the spa.

7. Which of the following information about health, sanitation, and facility security should be included in your policies and procedures manual?
   a) Current lifeguard schedule.
   b) A safety checklist of items to be inspected on a regular schedule.
   c) A checklist of items to be inspected immediately after the facility is closed, including security procedures.
   d) An outline of procedures to follow to maintain or repair broken fixtures or equipment.
   e) Cleaning procedures to follow and who is responsible for the cleaning.

8. Some common problem areas in aquatic facilities and waterfronts that need to be checked during safety inspections include—
   a) First aid stations.
   b) Beach area.
   c) Docks.
   d) Locker rooms and showers.
   e) Parking lots.
   f) Pool area.
   g) Spas and wading pools.

9. Which of the following items should be included in a first aid station at all times?
   a) Pens, pencils, and paper.
   b) Flashlight and extra batteries.
   c) Eye dressing pads.
   d) Splints.
   e) Long backboard with at least three straps and a commercial head immobilizer.
   f) Disposable latex gloves.

10. Which of the following electrical items could come in contact with the water?
    a) Pool vacuum cleaners.
    b) Underwater lighting.
    c) Automatic timing devices.
    d) Tape recorders.
    e) Pacemakers.

11. Which of the following precautions can be taken to prevent or decrease vandalism in an aquatic facility?
    a) Check the roof for soundness and secure all skylights.
    b) Make sure all windows and doors are securely locked every night.
    c) Check the walls and windows for deterioration or damage.
    d) Make sure the guard dogs are well fed.
    e) Extra night lights at vulnerable spots around the building will double and sometimes triple protection.

12. Match the type of lifeguard station with the advantage listed.
    Advantages:
    1. ___Better surveillance potential.
    2. ___Reach swimmers who need help more quickly.
    3. ___Quiet and effective disciplinary actions.
    Type of Lifeguard Station:
    a) Ground-level stations
    b) Elevated stations
    c) Boat stations

13. Match the type of surveillance coverage with the correct advantages and disadvantages. Note: each type of coverage will be used more than once.
    Advantages and Disadvantages:
    1. ___The lifeguard is required to observe a large area.
    2. ___It requires a smaller number of staff.
    3. ___Overlapping zones allow double coverage.
    4. ___Large facilities require more staff.
    5. ___The lifeguard may concentrate too much attention on the extreme boundaries of the area.
    6. ___Lifeguards concentrate on a limited area.
    7. ___Lifeguards may not scan their entire zone if its boundaries are not clearly marked.
    8. ___Lifeguards may be confused about their area of responsibility.
    Type of Surveillance Coverage:
    a) Zone coverage
    b) Total coverage

Circle *True* or *False*.

14. Lifeguards who move to new surveillance points at set times are more likely to become bored and lax in their surveillance. True or False?

See answers to study questions on page 120.

SELECTING LIFEGUARDS

4

Objectives

After reading this chapter, you should be able to—

1. Describe the head lifeguard's role in selecting lifeguards to work in the facility.
2. List at least three skill areas a lifeguard applicant should be tested on during the preemployment process.
3. Describe the head lifeguard's role in interviewing lifeguard applicants.
4. List five characteristics of an effective lifeguard.
5. Explain how behavioral interviewing techniques help assess an applicant's characteristics.
6. Define the key terms for this chapter.

Key Terms

Behavioral interviewing techniques: Asking an applicant to describe an event in his or her life.

Certification: A process in which a person demonstrates specific knowledge, competency, and skills and receives a certificate to that effect.

Preemployment test form: A form that documents an applicant's certification and test results before he or she becomes employed.

INTRODUCTION

As a head lifeguard, your role in selecting lifeguards for employment in your facility will vary among different facilities. In some small facilities, the head lifeguard may also be the facility manager, in which case, staff hiring may be done by him or her. In many facilities, however, the head lifeguard helps assess applicants, but management makes the final decision as to which applicants to hire. Either way, you need a clear understanding of your facility's needs and a lifeguard's required **competencies.** Work with your supervisor or personnel department to choose the best possible applicant.

THE SELECTION PROCESS

The selection process involves evaluating applicants in different ways. Applicants must meet age and certification requirements, demonstrate various competencies and knowledge, and have certain characteristics. As head lifeguard, you may be involved in interviewing applicants, screening their skills and knowledge, and checking required *certification.*

The **preemployment process** begins when an applicant fills out the application form for employment. This form contains personal information such as name, address, social security number, and telephone number. It also contains work-related information, such as the ap-

plicant's work experience, certification, and letters of recommendation.

Unless you hire the lifeguards at your facility, you may see the application form only before the preemployment testing and interviewing you will be involved in. Reviewing the application at this time helps you understand the applicant's work history, abilities, and certification. Knowing this information also helps you formulate questions for the interview. Because all information in the application is confidential, do not share it with anyone.

Your facility probably uses an applicant *preemployment test form* such as the one shown in Figure 4-1. This form documents certification and test results. The form typically includes the following:

• Applicant's name
• Certification dates in CPR, first aid, and lifeguarding (copies of certificates should be attached)
• Date and time of the preemployment test
• Facility administering preemployment test
• Personnel administering test(s)
• Score on written test of CPR, first aid, lifeguarding, and other questions related to the position
• Demonstrated lifeguarding skills such as rescue skills, first aid skills, and CPR

The preemployment test form should include an evaluation system for demonstrated skills. This may be a number scale ranging from unsatisfactory to excellent or a simple pass or fail. Appendix E is a sample preemployment test form.

figure 4-1 *A preemployment test form documents an applicant's certification and preemployment test results.*

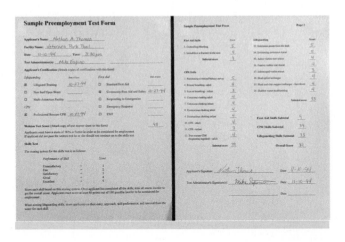

AGE AND CERTIFICATION REQUIREMENTS

Lifeguard age, level of training, and certification **criteria** are established by the facility and follow minimum standards outlined in state or local ordinances. For example, some facilities require that lifeguards must be at least 16 years old and have current certification in American Red Cross Lifeguard Training, American Red Cross Community First Aid and Safety, and American Red Cross CPR for the Professional Rescuer.

Before employment, lifeguard applicants must show proof of age and current certifications to meet all state, local, and facility requirements. Applicants should show their original certificates (Fig. 4-2). Be sure there are no signs of tampering with the certificates, such as date changes, overwriting, or other signs of changes or additions. Copies of certificates are usually filed in the facility personnel department or kept by management or the head lifeguard. All certifications should be kept current until the end of the employment period.

Year-round facilities typically have a system to monitor certification expiration dates. The head lifeguard can plan, update, or review lifeguards' training based on these expiration dates. The certificates from different organizations have different valid time periods, so you need to check the certification period, as well as state, local, and facility requirements.

As head lifeguard, you need to become familiar with the different types of certifications for lifeguards so that you can best conduct screening and assign lifeguard positions. Along with management, you should know what specific skills and knowledge are needed for different positions in the facility. Certain courses may not cover all the information and skills needed at your facility for any specific position. In this case, an individual with a certain kind of certification still may not have all the skills needed for the job. For example, a pool lifeguarding course does not provide the specific skills and knowledge a lifeguard needs to be fully effective at a waterfront area. You need to determine the applicant's level and type of training through interviewing and screening tests so that the individual can be assigned to a certain position or receive additional training. In-service training is always used to train staff in specific aspects and policies of the facility, but hiring applicants who already have the appropriate certification for the facility may reduce the amount of training you need to provide.

PREEMPLOYMENT TESTING

As a head lifeguard, you may also have a role in preemployment testing. This would include assessing and evaluating applicants' skills and knowledge to ensure they can do the job well. Many employers seek head lifeguards who are also lifeguarding instructors because instructors are trained in assessment and evaluation of skills.

Skills and competency screening

Current certification does not guarantee that the person has maintained his or her skills and knowledge. Therefore screening and testing are necessary before employment. You can assess knowledge through a written test. You can test decision-making skills by using scenarios or simulations in which the applicants must decide or act based on the situation.

How you organize this screening process depends on the number of candidates, the availability and type of testing space, and the availability of qualified staff to assist. You can test candidates at the same time or individually. You may wish to rotate a large group through the tests at separate stations if you have additional qualified

figure 4-2 *A lifeguard applicant should show proof of current certification before being offered employment.*

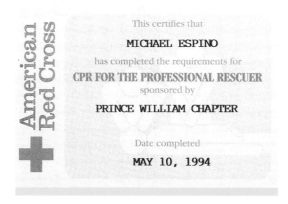

figure 4-3 *Lifeguard applicants' rescue skills should be tested during the preemployment process.*

Guidelines for Constructing Written Tests

To find out how well lifeguard applicants understand and retain what they have learned, an objective test works well. In an objective test, questions have right or wrong answers that do not involve interpretation. Objective tests usually use multiple choice, true or false, and fill-in questions. Often these tests are completely multiple choice. Objective tests are easy and quick to score with an answer key.

Following are principles for writing good objective test questions.

Multiple-choice test questions

Multiple-choice test questions begin with a statement or question and usually give a choice of four answers. Only one answer is correct; the others are called distractors. It may be an answer to a question or a completion of a statement.

1. Each question should test only one central idea or piece of information.
2. Each question should be independent of every other question. Do not link questions.
3. The information in one question should not help the person answer another question.
4. Write as clearly, simply, briefly, and correctly as possible.
5. Avoid negatively phrased questions. (Write "Which is part of a stride jump?" not "Which is not part of a stride jump?")
6. Be sure there is only one correct answer.
7. The wrong answers (distractors) should seem plausible to test takers who do not know the correct answer, but they should be clearly wrong or inadequate in some way.
8. Distractors may be common misconceptions, frequent mistakes, or other plausible but incorrect information.
9. Mix up the position of the correct answers in the order of distractors to avoid any pattern. For example, avoid a series of correct answers like this: a,b,c,d,a,b,c,d or c,d,b,a,c,d,b,a. If you use "all of the above" as a last choice of four possible answers, be sure it is not always a correct answer.

True-false test questions

Since **true-false test questions** carry a 50 percent chance of a correct answer, even with a guess, they are less useful. True-false questions are useful, however, when you give tests that the test takers score themselves to get a quick, rough picture of their learning.

1. Questions should deal with a single idea or piece of information.
2. Statements should be entirely true or entirely false, not partly true or partly false.
3. Include about equal numbers of true and false questions, but make sure correct answers do not fall in a pattern such as 1, 3, and 5 being *false* and 2, 4, and 6 being *true*.
4. Do not create false statements by inserting "not" into true statements.
5. Do not simply repeat textbook statements or minor variations of textbook statements.

Fill-in test questions

Fill-in test questions consist of a statement with a *key* word or phrase missing. The test taker inserts the appropriate word or phrase in an indicated blank space or on a line to complete the statement.

1. Phrase statements so that there is only one possible correct answer.
2. Phrase statements so that the test taker is clear as to how long and how precise the correct answer must be.
3. The answer should be a single word or short phrase.
4. Phrase your question so that the blank falls near the end of the question.
5. Do not include more than two blanks in one question.
6. Since some words and phrases have meanings almost identical to others, in your checking of the answers, be open to accepting alternative words or phrases as correct.

staff to help. In all cases, be sure testing is consistent among all candidates. Share the tests and results with management. Usually, you attach scores and times to the application form and discuss them with the candidate during the interview.

Rescue skills. Test all lifeguard applicants' rescue skills (Fig. 4-3, p. 53). Lifeguards need to be able to enter the water, swim to a victim, use equipment to rescue a victim, and move the victim to safety. You can use the rescue skills in the American Red Cross Lifeguard Training course for this skills screening. (See Appendix F for a list of these skills.)

First aid and CPR skills. Lifeguards must have a working knowledge of first aid and CPR. Since they watch over both adults and children, training in first aid and CPR should take this into consideration. You can use the first aid skills in the American Red Cross Lifeguard Training course and CPR for the Professional Rescuer course for first aid and CPR skills screening. (See Appendix F for a list of these skills.)

You can set up simulated situations to test applicants on their ability to make decisions and to rescue and care for victims (Fig. 4-4). The following are examples of such situations:

- A child runs on the deck, falls, and suffers abrasions on the legs and arms.
- A person appears to be suffering from a heat-related emergency.
- A near-drowning victim needs rescue breathing.
- An adult dives into the shallow water, hitting his head. He is conscious and breathing, but unable to move.
- A person collapses unconscious on the deck.

INTERVIEWING

Your role in interviewing applicants depends on the size and staffing of the facility and the policies of management. You may conduct one of several interviews with lifeguard applicants, or you may be the only person interviewing them. In some cases, you may not have an active role in the interviewing at all. Since you will supervise the lifeguards who are hired, the process works best when you are involved in it.

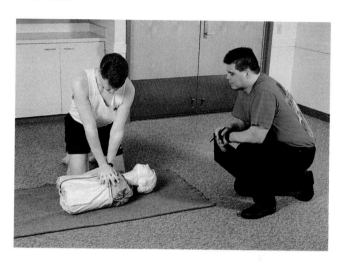

figure 4-4 *The preemployment process should also test the lifeguard's decision-making ability and the ability to care for a victim.*

figure 4-5 *Look for these characteristics during the lifeguard applicant's interview.*

- RELIABILITY
- DECISION MAKING
- COURTESY AND CONSISTENCY
- POSITIVE ATTITUDE
- PEOPLE SKILLS

In the interview, you determine whether the applicant has the personal characteristics needed to be an effective lifeguard. The interview also helps you see whether the person will fit in as a member of the lifeguard team. Before the interview, review the candidate's written and skill tests and identify any needs for additional training. Remember that if a lifeguard applicant is deficient in certain skills, you can give the needed training. Sometimes it is a good investment of time, effort, and money to give this training to a person who has the desired characteristics.

Lifeguards need the following characteristics to perform their jobs most effectively. In the interview, look for signs of these characteristics (Fig. 4-5).

Reliability

Lifeguards should arrive for work on time, assume their responsibilities, and accept assignments.

Decision making

Lifeguards should be able to make sound decisions in keeping with agency policies. They must be able to deal with difficult situations. The decisions a lifeguard makes may affect the entire facility staff.

Courtesy and consistency

Lifeguards should be firm, fair, consistent, and courteous when interacting with the public.

Positive attitude

The lifeguard should show his or her eagerness to act professionally at all times. Cooperating with other lifeguards in team efforts and following rules and regulations are important for the successful operation of the facility. The lifeguard should also show initiative in making constructive suggestions for better operations.

People skills

People skills include the ability to relate to others, effective communication skills, openness to new ideas, and the ability to take criticism.

Use *behavioral interviewing techniques* to help you assess these personal characteristics. These techniques involve asking applicants to describe events in their lives, referring to names, dates, places, numbers, and times. In your questions, use phrases such as "Give me

an example of . . .," " Tell me about a time when . . .," and "Describe a situation in which you . . . ." You can, for example, ask applicants to tell you about an emergency in which they were involved. Often the applicant has not had a lifeguard emergency, but you can ask about other life experiences that would show you how he or she might react in an emergency. You might ask, "Were you ever caring for a younger child when the child had an accident?" or "Have you ever been with a group of friends when someone got hurt? How did you react in the situation? What did you do? What steps did you take? How was the emergency resolved?" The applicants' answers may help you determine their ability to make a decision in an emergency or to react appropriately in a hectic situation.

For example, an applicant might say that while he or she was babysitting, the child fell and cut his arm. The applicant assessed the wound and determined that it was not deep, calmed the child, and put a bandage on the wound. Since the wound stopped bleeding with the bandage in place, he or she did not call for additional help but kept watching the child and the wound. Such an answer could show the applicant knows how to assess a situation and take appropriate steps.

You may also ask applicants if they have ever had to work or take a class with someone they didn't like. If the applicant had to work on a project or complete a task with such a person, ask, "How did you determine who would do what? Were you able to get the job done by yourselves without the boss or a teacher getting involved? Did you or the other person argue or refuse to complete the work?" Questions like these can help you assess the applicant's ability to be a team player or to deal with a difficult situation.

Following are other sample questions that can help you determine whether applicants have the right people skills:

- What accomplishments are you most proud of?
- Why do you want to work for our facility?
- How would our facility improve if you were hired?
- What would you do in a situation in which a 10-year-old is consistently ignoring a rule?
- What do you expect from those who supervise you?
- As our guests enter the facility, how would you make them feel welcome?
- What's your best experience in _____? (teaching children or caring for children, lifeguarding, interacting with adults or those in authority, etc.)
- What is the most important aspect of working with people?

A lifeguard who is hired after such an interview will understand that the facility values these people skills. Your interview lays a foundation for using people skills that you can continue to emphasize during orientation and in-service training.

The interview also gives the applicant more information about the job and its responsibilities. Give applicants a copy of the job description at the beginning of the preemployment process so that they know the requirements before proceeding to the screening and interviewing steps. In the interview, encourage applicants to ask questions about the job, the lifeguard's responsibilities, the facility's policies, and management's expectations. The applicant needs to feel comfortable with the job to fit into the organization.

When interviewing any applicant, you must also follow certain legal guidelines. You cannot ask any questions that could conceivably be discriminatory. You should be familiar with federal, state, and local legislation, including issues relating to the Americans with Disabilities Act. Appendix G gives guidelines for nondiscriminatory preemployment questions.

LIFEGUARD SELECTION

Once preemployment screening, testing, and interviewing are over, the decision is made about which applicants to hire as lifeguards. This decision depends on the applicants' previous experience, results of the preemployment written and skills tests, and the interviews. The facility may have other determining factors as well, such as the results of a drug test or physical examination. Facility policies outline the process by which an offer of employment is made and the details of establishing an employee relationship. You may have a large or small role in this process. Talk with your supervisor or personnel department to learn your exact role in the hiring of a new lifeguard and the procedures to follow in processing a new employee.

SUMMARY

To help choose the right lifeguard for your facility, understand both facility and lifeguard characteristics. Specific facility policies set employment criteria, develop application forms, and determine the content and use of written and practical tests. Be aware of state and local regulations and policies regarding staffing and facility management.

STUDY QUESTIONS

Circle the letter of the best answer or answers.

1. While trying to select lifeguards for an aquatic facility, a head lifeguard may be involved with—
   a) Interviewing applicants.
   b) Screening skills and knowledge.
   c) Checking required certification.
   d) Hiring an applicant.

2. A written test score should be included in the—
   a) Application form.
   b) Applicant preemployment test form.
   c) Certification test form.
   d) Skills test form.

3. The head lifeguard must check the expiration dates for employee certifications. These can vary as a result of—
   a) The issuing organization(s).
   b) The age of the lifeguard or employee.
   c) The type of facility involved.
   d) Local health department regulations.

4. Selecting a lifeguard candidate with the certification that is most appropriate to the needs of the facility—
   a) Eliminates the need for in-service training.
   b) Helps limit the amount of additional training needed.
   c) Is the most important factor in hiring a new lifeguard.
   d) All of the above.

5. The three skill areas a lifeguard should be tested on during the preemployment testing process are—
   a) Rescue skills, people skills, and CPR/first aid skills.
   b) CPR skills, first aid skills, and rescue skills.
   c) People skills, specific competencies, and rescue skills.
   d) Specific competencies, CPR/first aid skills, and people skills.

6. An interview with lifeguard applicants can help—
   a) Determine if an applicant has the necessary characteristics for effective lifeguarding.
   b) Evaluate the candidate's test results.
   c) Determine whether an individual will fit as a member of the lifeguard team.
   d) Identify additional training needs.

7. The following characteristics of a lifeguard are necessary for effective job performance:
   a) Reliability.
   b) Good decision-making skills.
   c) Strength.
   d) Courtesy and consistency.
   e) Positive attitude.
   f) Excellent rescue skills

8. Behavioral interviewing techniques can help assess—
   a) An applicant's ability to make a decision in an emergency.
   b) An applicant's ability to react appropriately in a hectic situation.
   c) An applicant's ability to be a team player.
   d) An applicant's ability to perform maintenance duties.

See answers to study questions on p. 120.

TRAINING

5

After reading this chapter, you should be able to—

1. List eight items to include in an orientation for new lifeguards.
2. Explain how to plan and schedule in-service training.
3. Describe five topic areas and skill practices that can be covered in in-service training.
4. Explain the four steps to use to give corrective feedback when evaluating a lifeguard's skills.
5. List five aspects of an emergency situation to focus on in a simulation.
6. Describe two methods for an in-service review of rules and regulations and policies and procedures.
7. Explain how to conduct new and review certification courses during in-service training.
8. Explain why lifeguards need to participate in a fitness program.
9. Explain how to help staff maintain their fitness at peak levels.
10. Define the key terms for this chapter.

In-service training: Scheduled staff meetings and practice sessions that cover lifeguarding information and skills.

Orientation: A meeting for familiarizing new employees with all aspects of their workplace and their job responsibilities.

Simulation: A lifelike teaching situation in which individuals or a whole team works to solve a given problem.

INTRODUCTION

Facility management is responsible for the on-going training of its lifeguards. As head lifeguard, your role in this training may include planning and conducting training sessions or assisting the facility manager in doing so. Training may be conducted before or during the season at seasonal facilities or throughout the year at year-round facilities. Since lifeguards need extensive technical skill and knowledge, as well as a clear understanding of their facility's policies and procedures, training sessions should cover key skills, facility procedures, and conditioning. Lifeguards' ability to react quickly and correctly develops and improves with experience, practice, and proper training.

ORIENTATION

New lifeguards must be thoroughly oriented to the facility and the job. As head lifeguard, you have a major role in this training. *Orientation* gives the new lifeguard his or her first impression of the job. The attitude the person forms at this time can last throughout his or her employment.

The orientation session should be businesslike, but it should also have a helpful and friendly atmosphere. Before conducting the orientation—

- Determine what information new lifeguards must have.
- Consider how long it will take to cover the material. Plan time for questions, discussion, breaks, and a tour of the facility.
- Have the appropriate forms, manuals, equipment, and supplies ready.
- Set up your training area so that it is conducive to learning; choose an area away from noise and other interruptions and distractions.
- Check the facility in advance to ensure everything is arranged as it is when lifeguards are on duty.
- Plan to present information using a variety of techniques such as demonstration, lecture, and group discussion.

The orientation should include some or all of the following elements:

- A personal welcome. New lifeguards should be made to feel comfortable. Introduce them to each other and to other management or staff present. Encourage them to feel that supervisors and management will help them adjust to the facility and job.
- Review of job descriptions and responsibilities. Employees should have a clear understanding of what is expected of them.
- Tour of the facility to view and discuss the following (Fig. 5-1, *A-D*):
  - Hazardous areas
  - Location of rescue equipment
  - Location of telephones and first aid supplies
  - Zones or areas lifeguards cover. Also explain the lifeguard rotation system
  - Location and meaning of facility signs
  - Lifeguard lounge or break area
- Discuss uniform and dress code requirements.
- Discuss personnel policies, including—
  - Promptness.
  - Call-in procedures.
  - Breaks.
  - Posting of schedules (Fig. 5-2).
  - Smoking policies.
  - Use of time cards.
  - Hours of work.
  - Pay schedule.
  - Use of telephones.
  - Benefits.
  - Safety policies.
  - Disciplinary action.
  - Methods of staff evaluation.
- Review communication techniques.
- Review emergency action plans, including a description of the facility's chain of command.
- Explain security systems.
- Review facility opening and closing procedures.
- Discuss public relations, including how to manage difficult or disorderly people.
- Review and discuss how to prevent disease transmission in an emergency when a lifeguard contacts another person's bodily fluids.
- Review and discuss weather-related problems.
- Review maintenance procedures, including water chemistry and procedures, such as cleaning filters, vacuuming, and extracting human waste from the pool (if included in the lifeguard's job description).
- Discuss proper handling of chemicals and related safety procedures (if included in the lifeguard's job description).
- Give an overview of any additional aspects of facility operations.
- Discuss other activities, facility rules, and specific facility policies and procedures.

figure 5-1 *During a lifeguard orientation, tour the facility and point out and discuss the following:* **A,** *hazardous areas,* **B,** *location of rescue equipment,* **C,** *location of first aid supplies, and* **D,** *facility signs.*

A

B

C

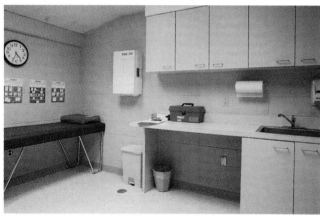

D

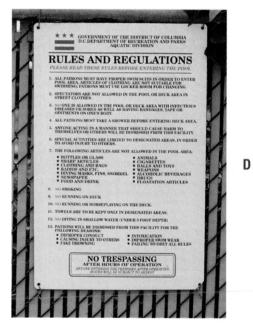

figure 5-2 *Discuss the posting of lifeguard schedules during a lifeguard orientation.*

New lifeguards should leave the orientation session clearly understanding what is expected of them. New lifeguards should also feel help is available if they need it. Since you begin your team building with this session, you want to appear professional yet friendly and accessible.

IN-SERVICE TRAINING

n-service training should occur often throughout the season or year, with a session at least once a month (Fig. 5-3). When planning and scheduling training sessions, consider what hours are available at the facility and when lifeguards are available. The facility's management may insist that the facility does not close for training during normal operating hours. In such a case, your in-service training has to be scheduled when the facility is closed.

To build a strong, effective, and well-informed lifeguarding team, you must also plan training sessions at a time when all lifeguards can attend. At times this is difficult because staff may have previously planned activities or unavoidable circumstances may come up, such as illness or a death in the family. If some staff cannot attend, arrange to meet with them soon after the session so that you can go over the material with them. Remember, lifeguards have a professional responsibility to attend in-service training; your responsibility is to remind them of this professional commitment to attend.

figure 5-3 *In-service training provides lifeguards the opportunity to stay informed and to practice and update rescue skills.*

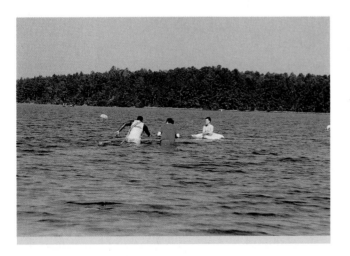

Other factors influence what training sessions you offer and how you schedule, including—

- How many lifeguards are employed.
- Amounts and types of equipment available.
- Facility budget.
- Weather conditions (at outdoor facilities).

Keep in mind during lifeguard in-service training-sessions that include staff entering the water that *a non-participating lifeguard should always be on surveillance duty.*

With any in-service training, first plan the goals and the objectives for the session. Structure in-service training to cover topics and skills that help the lifeguard staff grow professionally. Do not have a training session just for the sake of having one. If you don't have clear goals and objectives, your lifeguards may feel the session was a waste of time and served no purpose. This could hurt attendance at future sessions or, even worse, affect the functioning of the lifeguard team as a whole.

Select topics or skill practices to enhance the lifeguards' skills, knowledge, and enthusiasm. These could include—

- Evaluation of lifeguarding skills.
- Review and practice of the emergency action procedures.
- Review of the facility's rules and regulations.
- Review of the facility's policies and procedures.
- Updates on current legislation and upcoming special events.
- Patron relations.
- Certification training.
- Lifeguard fitness and conditioning.

Make every effort to ensure your in-service training is fun, informative, and challenging. Be creative in how you conduct the training. For example, you may bring in a guest speaker to talk about a current trend in lifeguarding, you may divide your lifeguards into teams and have a lifeguarding competition, you may have a simulated emergency involving other agencies, such as EMS, and you may give training in other aquatic areas, such as SCUBA, to help your lifeguards understand the programs they lifeguard.

Evaluation of staff lifeguard skills

Before being hired, your new lifeguards were tested on many lifeguarding skills. In these screening sessions, you may have seen a need for more training or skill improvement. New lifeguards may also need to improve or learn other skills. You may have year-round or returning staff with training needs. For all these reasons, in-service training should periodically evaluate the skills of all lifeguards. The evaluation session gives you a clear idea of what training or skills practice lifeguards need.

You and the facility manager should compile a list of lifeguarding skills needed at the facility. Some skills may be specific for the facility, such as certain spinal injury management procedures at a waterpark or use of a rescue board at a waterfront facility. First aid and CPR skills should also be included. See Appendix F for a sample list of skills.

Before evaluating lifeguards' skills, organize them for effective skill practice and performance. Use a pattern of class organization, a formation that best gives lifeguards the opportunity to practice and develop the desired skill. Become familiar with common patterns of class organization, such as for group discussions, demonstrations, drills in which the participants remain in one spot (static

drills), and drills in which the participants move from one point to another (fluid drills). You can also modify these by using simulations for some skills. Sample patterns of class organization are on pages 64 and 65.

Using your chosen pattern of organization, evaluate your lifeguards on each skill. Look for correct performance, and note any critical errors. Have a system for listing the criteria for each skill and noting errors (Fig. 5-4). If you are an American Red Cross Lifeguarding Instructor, you can refer to your *Lifeguarding Instructor's Manual* for lists of criteria for skills or talk to someone who is an American Red Cross Lifeguarding Instructor for help in identifying these criteria. Other resources include the *American Red Cross Lifeguarding Today* textbook and the *American Red Cross Lifeguarding Today* video.

When evaluating skills, be sure to give the lifeguards feedback on their performance. Focus on the skill, not the person performing it, so that the lifeguard does not perceive the feedback negatively. Follow these steps to give corrective feedback:

1 Describe what you observed. Tell the lifeguard what he or she was doing correctly, then describe the critical errors. Do not overwhelm the lifeguard with a long list of problems.

2 Make specific suggestions as to how to improve.

3 Allow time for questions or clarification.

4 Give an opportunity to practice correctly.

As in any training and evaluation session, ensure the safety of all participants. You may need additional help during evaluation activities. With a large group and no additional help, break the lifeguards into smaller groups. If you have help, give the helpers consistent, clear guidelines for evaluating the skills.

Emergency procedures

Emergencies can happen even at a well-guarded facility. To make sure any emergency will be handled effectively, review the facility's emergency action plans with your staff in periodic in-service training sessions. Have your lifeguards walk through the emergency action plans for different types of emergencies. Discuss with them the importance of emergency action plans and how

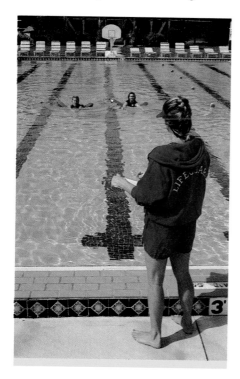

figure 5-4 *Lifeguard skills can be evaluated during in-service training.*

Patterns of Class Organization

Use patterns of class organization to make sure all lifeguards can practice their skills effectively. To organize the group for optimal learning and evaluation, physically arrange the group so that—

• Everyone's safety is ensured.
• Everyone can hear and see instructions and demonstrations.
• Everyone has an opportunity for sufficient practice.
• Everyone has an opportunity to be checked for skill improvement.

Demonstrations

When you demonstrate a skill either on land or in the water, be sure all lifeguards are close enough and positioned so that everyone can see. For a demonstration of a moving skill in water, lifeguards can stand in a single line along the pool edge (Fig. A-1). For a demonstration of a stationary skill in water, lifeguards can stand or sit in an L formation at the corner of the pool (Fig. A-2) or in parallel (Fig. A-3) or multiple lines (Fig. A-4).

Static drills

In a static drill, skills are practiced in one spot. Static drills work well for skills like kicking on the wall, treading water, and practicing an isolated part of a skill without moving through the water. Lifeguards can be in any safe arrangement along the sides of the pool, standing in lines, or randomly scattered, depending on your area. Position yourself where you can see all lifeguards from above at all times, such as on the deck. Looking down through the water gives the best view of the lifeguards' performance.

Fluid drills

In a fluid drill, lifeguards move through the water, such as when practicing an approach or swimming for fitness conditioning. Vary the type and formation of drills to keep the practice interesting and help lifeguards meet their goals. Vary the drills depending on these factors:

• Lifeguards' skill proficiency
• Lifeguards' physical condition
• The intensity level of each drill
• The frequency and length of rest periods

Individual instruction

Observe your lifeguards one at a time when you need to take extra safety considerations. Carefully monitor skills such as entering the water from a height (compact jump) or a submerged victim rescue. Because giving feedback to one lifeguard at a time is inefficient for larger groups, have another activity for the rest of the group. For example, they can practice a previously learned rescue skill related to the skill you are observing individually or leading up to it.

A-1

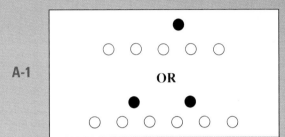

Samples of a single line formation. Solid dots show location of instructors.

A-2

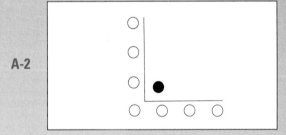

"L" formation.

A-3

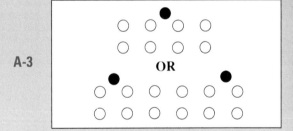

Samples of parallel lines.

A-4

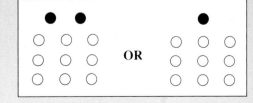

Samples of multiple lines.

Wave formation

In a wave formation, one group follows another. You can divide a large group into smaller units for the best supervised practice. Lifeguards count off by number and form groups, and each group then performs as a unit. The units remain in single lines, with one unit behind the other. You signal the first unit to start swimming. The next unit in line starts when the unit ahead reaches a certain spot. This method lets you watch smaller groups and give better feedback. It also makes better use of a small practice area (Fig. B).

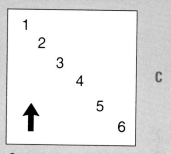

Wave pattern. Arrow indicates direction of travel.

Stagger formation

In the stagger formation the whole group remains in a single line. You signal the first lifeguard in line to start swimming. The next lifeguard in line starts when the lifeguard ahead reaches a certain spot. This lets you follow the progress of each lifeguard for a few body lengths. It also lets you speak to each lifeguard as he or she finishes the swim or skill and gives you enough time to watch the next lifeguard. This method allows a large amount of practice time on a skill, as well as individual feedback. Lifeguards also get a short rest period while they

Stagger pattern. Arrow indicates direction of travel.

Circle swimming

For fitness training, lifeguards may use the pool lanes. Have them keep to the right and remain in the same lane while they turn and continue swimming. Another option is a circuit swim, in which the lifeguards start in one lane and then move over a lane to swim in the other direction (always keeping to the right side of the lane). You can continue this pattern so that the lifeguards use all the available lanes. With this method, you can stop any lifeguard at any time to make corrections and give feedback (Fig. D).

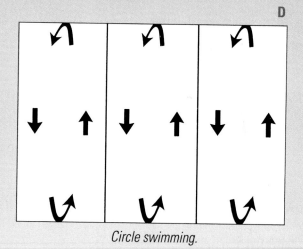

Circle swimming.

Paired coaching

Lifeguards can effectively observe and help each other. Lifeguards learn better by observing others along with being observed themselves.

Summary of other options

The more flexibility and variety you can build into your skills practice, the more successful and effective this in-service training will be. You can alternate among perimeter, circle, stagger, diagonal, and other formation drills. Be creative in using whatever patterns the pool permits.

each lifeguard plays an essential role in the success of a plan. Talk about victim recognition, lifeguard reaction time, backup availability, and available support personnel. You may also want to discuss how life-threatening and nonlife-threatening emergencies affect the action plan.

Procedures for handling emergencies must be practiced often. A *simulation* of an emergency situation, such as a victim with a possible spinal injury, is an excellent way to ensure the lifeguards can follow the emergency action plan (Fig. 5-5). When planning an emergency simulation, you may want to involve EMS personnel in the training. This helps both your lifeguards and EMS personnel better understand each other's roles and responsibilities during an actual emergency. In your simulation, concentrate on the following five aspects of an emergency situation:

1 **Identification of situation.** Examples include victim in distress, victim drowning, spinal injury, and facility-related situations such as exposure to chemicals.

2 **Individual responsibilities.**

3 **Emergency communications.**

4 **Backup coverage.**

5 **Records and reports.**

After the simulation, evaluate the actions of all staff and EMS personnel involved. This helps you, your lifeguards, and EMS personnel identify strengths to build upon and problems to correct.

Many different types of emergencies can occur at any facility, and each type of emergency has its own plan for procedures. Be sure to vary emergency situations in each training session.

Rules and regulations

Periodically, you need to review facility rules and regulations with lifeguards. Lifeguards and patrons tend to forget some rules over the course of a season. Use a variety of methods to review this material with lifeguards during in-service training sessions.

One review method begins with giving a list of the facility's rules and regulations to the lifeguards. Read and discuss the rules while the lifeguards follow along on their copies (Fig. 5-6). Give examples of behaviors that break each of the rules. Explain what disciplinary actions are appropriate for each **infraction.**

When reviewing rules and regulations, emphasize that rules should be enforced consistently. Disciplinary action must be fair and consistent, following the facility's procedures.

Explain how lifeguards should deal with patrons who break a rule. Lifeguards should know whom to contact for help, especially for removing from the facility a patron who continues to break rules.

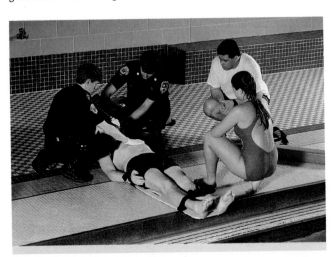

figure 5-5 *Simulated emergencies help prepare your lifeguards for real emergencies.*

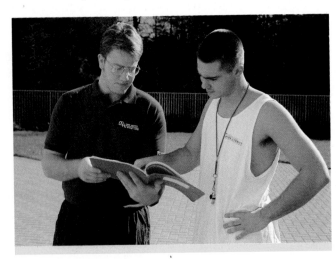

figure 5-6 *Periodically review the facility's rules and regulations with your lifeguards.*

You can also use verbal quizzes to review rules and evaluate how well the lifeguards know the rules, how to enforce them, and what disciplinary action to use. Following is a method you can use:

1 **Write several questions, each one on a separate piece of paper, and fold the paper.**

2 **Put the questions in a container and mix them up.**

3 **With all lifeguards present, have each lifeguard draw a question from the container.**

4 **For each question, the lifeguard first answers the question verbally, and then the entire group discusses it.**

5 **Continue this procedure until all questions have been answered and discussed.**

You can develop other methods and formats for reviewing rules and regulations. No matter what method you use, be sure your lifeguards understand the reasons for the rules and are consistent in enforcing them.

Policies and procedures

Lifeguards also tend to forget some of the facility's policies and procedures during the course of a year or season. For example, some lifeguards may begin to use the telephone for personal calls instead of only for official use.

To provide a "friendly reminder" for policies such as telephone use, you can review the facility policies. Review such policies and procedures during in-service training using any method described or your own method.

In addition to current policies and procedures, you may also have to present new policies and procedures at the facility. Any new policy or procedure may have an impact on lifeguards, and you need to explain how it will affect them.

Legislation

Many national, state, and local laws and regulations affect lifeguarding. Laws and regulations such as the **Occupational Safety and Health Administration's (OSHA)** bloodborne and airborne pathogens regulations can directly affect lifeguarding staff. Some laws and reg-

ulations require you to give specialized training, such as additional first aid training. If you cannot give this training yourself, you may need to bring in experts in that field.

As head lifeguard, you should become familiar with all laws and regulations that affect you and your lifeguarding staff. Talk to your facility manager, or contact your state health department and your regional OSHA office. Appendix H lists addresses for state health departments and regional OSHA offices.

Special events

Lifeguards need to know about future events planned for the facility. Post events with dates in the facility office in a list or on a calendar. Reviewing upcoming special events during in-service training helps prepare lifeguard staff.

For special events, lifeguard location, surveillance, rotation, and zone of coverage may differ from those of the day-to-day operations. Give written instructions to the lifeguards to explain the specific changes from normal policies. Go over these instructions with your lifeguards because they need a thorough understanding of their responsibilities for the special event. Give information about who is involved in the event, such as competitive swimmers, disabled patrons, or SCUBA classes.

If you can, give your lifeguards specialized training for the upcoming activity. For example, for lifeguarding a SCUBA class, the lifeguard would benefit from basic SCUBA training. For lifeguarding a competitive swimming event, the lifeguard would benefit from the American Red Cross Safety Training for Swim Coaches course. Any other training related to the upcoming event helps lifeguards be prepared for specific safety factors during that activity.

Patron relations

Although preventing emergencies and ensuring the safety of patrons is the lifeguard's primary responsibility, customer service is also important. How patrons view the lifeguard affects how well the lifeguard can do his or her job. For example, the way a lifeguard talks about safety rules affects how seriously patrons adhere to them. Your role as head lifeguard includes providing customer service training and monitoring how the staff gives that service.

The following tips will help you train your lifeguards in customer service.

- *Give efficient service.* If you can give the information or directions instead of sending the patron elsewhere, you save time and also give a good impression of being knowledgeable and helpful.
- *Give an impression of helpfulness.* When not on surveillance, walk with the patron or find someone to show the way when giving directions rather than just pointing.
- *Use a team philosophy.* One lifeguard can help another staff member or give the patron more information.
- *Show genuine interest in patrons.* Initiate the contact with patrons who seem to need help; use polite terms such as Sir or Ms.; and look interested, concerned, and friendly.
- *Answer requests promptly.* If you cannot handle the question or situation, notify the head lifeguard, another staff member, or the facility manager immediately.
- *Give personalized service.* Explain rules and reasons for them, and be courteous when enforcing policies.
- *Do not abuse your authority.* Be fair and consistent in rule enforcement and handling difficult situations.
- *Be thoroughly familiar with facility operations and policies.* You must be able to give up-to-date, accurate information and know potential problem areas.
- *Be professional.* Be well groomed, and avoid unnecessary talking and gossiping while on duty.

In your customer service training, include opportunities for staff to role play given situations. For example, ask staff to give instructions to a young child or directions to an adult who does not speak English. Using simulations of patrons who are uncooperative or potentially violent helps lifeguards learn how to be strict and assertive yet still ensure the safety of other patrons. Acting out a scenario involving a patron who unintentionally violates a rule helps lifeguards learn how to be positive and non-offensive in communication.

Everyone in the facility benefits from good customer service. Complaints are fewer, patrons are happier and more likely to return, and staff have pride in the organization. Making employees feel they are valued will benefit customer service and morale. The lifeguards' positive attitude about their role will transfer to the public. A lifeguard who feels valued is more likely to value patrons.

Professional development

In-service training is also an excellent way to give new and review certification courses to your staff. These courses can range from first aid training to instructor level certification in specialty areas.

Consider the following when planning certification in-service training:

- Certification training can take much time, but don't ignore a course just because it does not fit into an allotted time period. A longer course can be spread out through several in-service training sessions.
- If you are not certified to teach a particular course, find someone who is. You may already have a certified person on your staff; if not, contact your local unit of the American Red Cross for help in locating an instructor.

Giving new certification courses to lifeguards is a great way to help them grow professionally. These courses can include—

- New training required by federal and state regulations, such as bloodborne pathogen training.
- Training to expand current knowledge and abilities. If your lifeguards are currently trained in first aid, you may want to give them a higher level of training, such as the American Red Cross Emergency Response course (Fig. 5-7).

figure 5-7 *Expand your lifeguards' knowledge by providing a higher level of training, such as the American Red Cross Emergency Response course.*

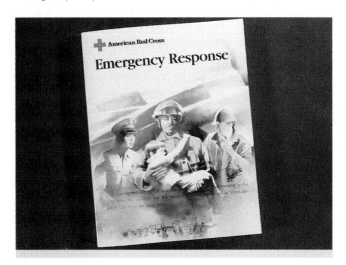

In addition to the Head Lifeguard course, the American Red Cross offers several courses you can use for in-service training. These include—

- **American Red Cross Emergency Response.**
- **American Red Cross Oxygen Administration module.**
- **American Red Cross Preventing Disease Transmission module.**
- **American Red Cross Waterpark Lifeguarding module.**
- **American Red Cross Waterfront Lifeguarding module.**
- **American Red Cross Safety Training for Swim Coaches.**
- **American Red Cross Water Safety Instructor.**
- **American Red Cross Instructor courses in First Aid, CPR, and Lifeguard Training.**

For further information on these courses, contact your local unit of the American Red Cross.

If your staff's certifications in lifeguard training, CPR, and first aid are about to expire, offer review courses through in-service training. This way you can update everyone at the same time, which helps you prepare a maintenance schedule for staff certifications.

DEVELOPING A LIFEGUARD FITNESS PROGRAM

You may be responsible for preparing lifeguards for situations in which they have to swim quickly to a victim but still retain energy to make the rescue, bring the victim to safety, and perform CPR or rescue breathing if necessary. To help your lifeguards stay fit to do this, you may develop a fitness program as part of your training (Fig. 5-8).

Two major systems supply energy to the body's muscles. The **anaerobic** (without oxygen) **energy system** uses the quickest source of energy—sugars and carbohydrates in the body—for muscular activity. The anaerobic energy system is the primary source of energy for **anaerobic exercise** or activity. Anaerobic activity is short-term, intense activity at a rate faster than the body can supply oxygen consistently.

For longer-lasting activity, the **aerobic** (oxygen-using) **energy system** gives the muscles energy. This system uses the carbohydrates, fats, and proteins in the body for energy. The body uses this system for **aerobic exercise** or activity. This is sustained, rhythmic exercise that requires additional effort by the heart and lungs to meet the muscles' increased demand for oxygen.

Which energy system the body uses in an activity depends on how long and intense the activity is. Training has benefits for both energy systems. To improve the anaerobic energy system, high-intensity, short-duration training is needed, such as with a series of high-speed, short-distance **sprints** with long rest periods in between each to allow the body to recover before the next exercise. An example of this training would be a series of ten 25-yard sprints with 30 to 60 seconds of rest between sprints. This allows the system to recharge before the next swimming exercise.

Improvements to the aerobic energy system require continuous, low- to moderate-intensity training. You can train the aerobic system by distance swimming at a moderate but steady pace, such as swimming 500 yards in under 10 minutes. You can also use medium distance swims (50-100 yards) mixed with shorter, faster swims

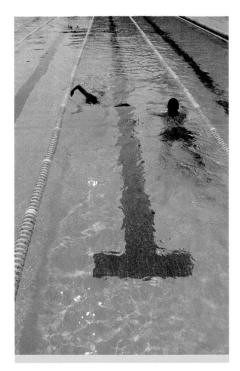

figure 5-8 *A fitness program helps prepare lifeguards to respond immediately to an emergency.*

(25 yards). One example is to swim 500 yards in the following format:

Length	Effort	Length	Effort
1	easy	3	easy
1	hard	1	hard
2	easy	2	easy
1	hard	1	hard
3	easy	1	easy
1	hard	3	lengths cool-down

Total 500 yards

Rather than using sprint training at the start of the season, it is better to first improve the lifeguards' overall fitness with steady long-distance training. As the lifeguards' fitness improves, introduce medium-to-fast-pace swims with plenty of rest and later, fast-pace swims with short rest periods. Wait until the lifeguards establish a good aerobic training base before introducing faster-pace workouts.

Your type of facility should affect how you design training sessions. For example, emphasize short sprints for a small pool, short and medium sprints for a larger facility, and long-distance training at a waterfront.

Since the muscles should always be stretched before and after swimming, start and end all sessions with a set of stretching exercises. The *American Red Cross Swimming and Diving* textbook and the *American Red Cross Aqua Fitness* booklet both have additional suggestions and information on warm-up and cool-down practices.

Following are examples of training sets for short and medium sprints and longer swims:

Short Distance Sprints

4 × 50 yards   25 yards freestyle or breaststroke sprint, 25 yards swimming while towing a 10-lb brick, on a 1:45 interval. Have two bricks per lane, with two swimmers each starting from opposite sides of the pool.

Medium Distance Sprints

4 × 100 yards   75 yards freestyle or breaststroke sprint, 25 yards sidestroke, on a 3:00 interval.

Long Distance Swims

100-200-300-200-100 yards: Freestyle, with a 20-second rest between distances.

The *American Red Cross Swimming and Diving* textbook provides further information on workout techniques. You can also talk with a local competitive swimming coach for ideas for suggested swimming workouts. A coach may suggest varying workout intervals, practice sets, and training tips.

Conditioning

One of your goals is to help lifeguards maintain their fitness at peak levels. Fitness training can be part of your in-service training program, but conditioning should be ongoing throughout the season or year. Have your lifeguards continue with their conditioning by encouraging them to swim on their own time, such as before or after their shifts or during lunch breaks.

A technique you can use to motivate lifeguards is to reward them for participating in in-service fitness workouts and ongoing conditioning training. Keep records of the number of yards each person swims during training periods, then reward the lifeguard who completes the most yards. This reward can be taking him or her to lunch at a favorite restaurant or giving a certificate of achievement at the end of the training period. (Other incentives are discussed in Chapter 6.)

Post a chart that shows the yards lifeguards swim in their workouts, along with a space for the initials of whoever witnesses the workout. This witness can be another lifeguard on duty during the workout. This way, you have an accurate record of who is performing their training, recognizable goals of performance, and easy tracking for lifeguards who are competing to swim the most yards. Post this chart in the facility office for easy access by all staff. You can use the *American Red Cross Aquatic Exercise Fitness Chart* for tracking yards (Fig. 5-9).

figure 5-9 *The American Red Cross Aquatic Exercise Chart.*

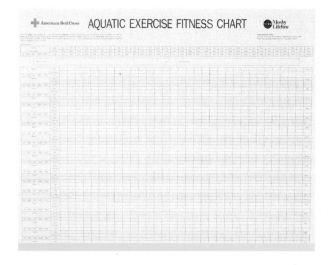

Lifeguard Competitions

Each year, hundreds of thousands of lifeguards are assigned to aquatic facilities that range from swimming pools to waterparks and waterfronts to ocean beaches. These lifeguards are charged with an enormous safety responsibility requiring high proficiency with rescue skills that are sometimes highly technical.

Maintaining a high proficiency in lifeguard skills requires hours of training. Tests of these skills may come in various forms, from an unannounced drill to an actual rescue. However, many facilities have found a more motivating way to ensure proficiency . . . the LIFEGUARD COMPETITION.

Competitions create motivation, enthusiasm, and an appreciation for lifeguards' responsibilities and activities. Participation in lifeguard competitions can benefit both an individual lifeguard and an aquatic facility. A lifeguard benefits by being able to train individually and sharpen his or her skills for a specific end result, not one that may or may not happen, as in a rescue situation. For example, a lifeguard learns how to perform CPR but may never have the occasion to use it. In a lifeguard competition, a lifeguard has the opportunity to perform the skill under competitive conditions while being subjectively evaluated against his or her peers. Lifeguards may also compete as a lifeguard team, which requires a coordinated effort by all team members to be successful. This can help build a sense of team spirit and pride.

Facilities benefit by having a well-trained, motivated staff that truly works as a team. The public relations aspect cannot be ignored either. Lifeguard competitions are an effective means of promoting a facility and can result in future employees being recruited. Patrons who use facilities that have lifeguard competitions frequently find a more professional operation as a result of the work put into competition preparation and participation.

Lifeguard competition events may be tailored to include any of the skills required of lifeguards. These may include physical skill events, such as swimming, equipment skill events, such as using rescue tubes or buoys, and specific skill events, such as CPR and spinal injury management. Lifeguards can participate in the events individually or as a member of a team relay. Events may be scored by times or by judges.

Lifeguard competitions are becoming more and more popular. Many competitions are promoted in aquatic journals, through professional organizations, or by word of mouth. As more and more interest is generated, more and more competitions will become available. Lifeguard competitions are a great way for lifeguards to ensure they have mastered skills while having some fun as well.

Chris Moler/Photographer

Some facilities require that lifeguards participate in a conditioning program as part of their job responsibilities. As head lifeguard, you may be responsible for suggesting swim workouts. Require a minimum number of yards of each lifeguard throughout the season. For example, if a minimum of 1000 yards a week is required, lifeguards may complete this in stages or all at one time, as long as it is completed and recorded every week.

IN-SERVICE TRAINING REPORTS

Keep records on all in-service training sessions, including the following:

- Date, time, and location
- Names of instructors/facilitators
- Subjects covered
- Names of attendees and their signatures

The facility should file and maintain in-service training records. Keep these records on file for at least 3 years for future reference and inspection. Appendix I is a sample in-service training record form.

SUMMARY

As head lifeguard, one of your key responsibilities is to plan and conduct in-service training for the lifeguards. Your evaluations of new lifeguards will help you identify skills needing additional training. Your experience and the needs of the facility will tell you what lifeguards need to know to effectively perform their duties. In-service training to provide these skills and that knowledge is a vital component of any safe and well-managed facility.

STUDY QUESTIONS

Circle the letter of the best answer or answers.

1. Which of the following could be included in an orientation for new lifeguards?
   a) Have the appropriate forms, manuals, equipment, and supplies ready.
   b) Make the employees feel welcome.
   c) Give new lifeguards a tour of the facility.
   d) Review and discuss uniform and dress code requirements.
   e) Provide in-service training.
   f) Give an overview of aspects of facility operations.

2. Which of the following are considerations for conducting in-service training?
   a) At least two in-service trainings per month.
   b) Availability of the lifeguarding staff.
   c) Facility budget.
   d) Weather conditions.
   e) A non-participating lifeguard on duty during training.

3. Topics and skill practices that could be included in an in-service training session include—
   a) Review of emergency action procedures.
   b) Review of rules and regulations.
   c) Certification trainings.
   d) Lifeguard fitness.
   e) Patron relations.
   f) New lifeguard orientation.

4. The steps to follow when giving constructive feedback to a lifeguard include—
   a) Describe what you have observed. First discuss what was performed correctly, then focus on critical errors.
   b) Provide the lifeguard with a long list of problems.
   c) Offer specific suggestions as to how to improve the performance.
   d) First point out all mistakes made, then focus on what was performed correctly.
   e) Allow time for questions or clarification.

5. Possible areas of concentration for an emergency situation simulation include—
   a) Identification of the situation.
   b) Emergency calls and signals.
   c) Review of rules and regulations.
   d) Records and reports.
   e) Dress code and professional appearance.
   f) Back-up systems.

6. Which of the following customer service tips can help improve patron relations at the facility?
   a) Give efficient service.
   b) Be helpful.
   c) Show interest in the patron.
   d) Be authoritative.
   e) Be professional.

7. Short-term, intense exercise is known as—
   a) Aerobic exercise.
   b) Anaerobic exercise.
   c) High-impact exercise.
   d) Short-term exercise.

8. The best way to help lifeguards maintain peak fitness levels is to—
   a) Reward them for participating in in-service fitness workouts.
   b) Discipline them for not participating in in-service fitness workouts.
   c) Provide ongoing fitness training and conditioning throughout the season or year.
   d) Have them swim for 30 minutes once a month.

See answers to study questions on p. 120.

BUILDING A LIFEGUARD TEAM

6

After reading this chapter, you should be able to—

1. Describe the head lifeguard's role as liaison between management and lifeguards.
2. Explain how a head lifeguard's leadership style affects the lifeguard team.
3. Describe three benefits of teamwork.
4. Explain how developing and accomplishing goals benefits a lifeguard team.
5. Describe five tips a head lifeguard can use for effective communication.
6. Describe the six-step approach for solving problems.
7. Explain the difference between delegating a responsibility and assigning a task.
8. Explain how recognition can motivate members of a lifeguard team.
9. Describe seven techniques for building a lifeguard team and improving leadership skills.
10. Explain how to correct a lifeguard's problem behavior.
11. Explain the need for and purpose of evaluating lifeguards.
12. Describe at least eight criteria for evaluating lifeguards.
13. Define the key terms for this chapter.

Communication: The process of passing information or ideas from one individual to another.

Delegation: The process of entrusting others with tasks for which you are responsible.

Leadership style: The manner in which one person interacts with and leads other people.

Lifeguard evaluation form: A form used to evaluate and document a lifeguard's performance level.

Performance evaluation: A process that determines how well an individual is performing his or her job duties.

Performance level: The ability to execute skills and demonstrate knowledge relative to the standards and expectations of the job.

Problem-solving skills: The ability to develop effective solutions for difficult situations.

S.M.A.R.T. goal: A goal that is Specific, Measurable, Attainable, Relevant, and Time oriented.

Teamwork: A shared sense of spirit in a group of individuals.

INTRODUCTION

Your position as head lifeguard includes a role as leader of the lifeguard team. In this role, you function as liaison between the lifeguards and the management of the facility, and you develop and use your leadership style to build the team and keep it working well. This chapter discusses leadership skills you can use for developing the lifeguard team and motivating lifeguards to give their best. As team leader, you also have a supervisory role to help lifeguards improve their performance, to correct a problem behavior, and to conduct periodic performance evaluations.

LIAISON WITH MANAGEMENT

One of your responsibilities as the head lifeguard is to serve as a liaison with management. You bring to the manager issues that lifeguards bring to your attention. The facility manager needs to know about any major problems and must be kept up to date on how well the facility is operating. For example, you bring major maintenance problems, unresolved conflicts, serious difficulties with patrons, and all serious emergencies to the attention of management.

Try to have periodic meetings with your supervisor to keep him or her informed, and be sure to communicate positive results and your team's successes, as well as any problems. Be specific in describing the steps you and the lifeguards are taking. Ask your supervisor for ideas and his or her perspective on how you and your lifeguards are doing.

Just as you represent the lifeguards to management, you represent management to the lifeguards. You therefore need a clear understanding of management's philosophy and the facility's policies so that you can communicate them to the lifeguard staff. Your goal is to support management while maintaining the trust and confidence of the lifeguards. Lifeguards must feel comfortable sharing information with you. Lifeguards' impression of management often depends on the image you present. Strive to be professional and trustworthy for both management and the lifeguards you supervise.

In addition, show support for your supervisor. If the supervisor suggests an idea at a lifeguard team meeting, don't contradict your supervisor outright or say that the group can come up with something better. Be diplomatic. You can acknowledge your supervisor's idea and then discuss it as a group.

Follow three general guidelines in your interactions with your supervisor and the lifeguards:

1 Always keep the focus on the issue or problem rather than the person involved.

2 Recognize and support the self-esteem and self-confidence of others.

3 Work to maintain good relationships with those above and below you in the facility's chain of command.

LEADERSHIP STYLE

Leadership style is a key factor in developing a lifeguard team. Leadership style involves the way you interact with and lead the lifeguards. Your leadership style can either help you and the lifeguard team be successful or cause frustration and conflict.

Leadership style depends on your unique personality and experience. Successful leaders recognize problems or conflicts and use the style that will work best in the particular situation, depending on their personality and the needs of the facility. Some leaders are very democratic and discuss every issue with all those they lead before making a decision. Others may seek input from select individuals and make a decision. Still other leaders may make all decisions by themselves. No one style is automatically right or wrong in all situations. Each can have its advantages and disadvantages.

For example, the facility may be about to issue new t-shirts as part of the lifeguards' uniform. The head lifeguard might choose the color of the new shirts or may let the lifeguards decide as a group. Neither approach is better. Even if the head lifeguard decides to let the whole team decide, he or she may have to step in and make the decision if the group cannot reach agreement. As another example, in developing the schedule the head lifeguard may first call for volunteers for each shift, but if no one volunteers for the early shift, he or she will have to make the decision as the leader of the team.

As you take on your head lifeguard responsibilities, be aware that you can lead in different ways. You will learn what feels comfortable, as well as what works for you in a particular situation. Try to develop a style that works best for the ongoing development of your lifeguard team.

DEVELOPING THE LIFEGUARD TEAM

Your supervisor in the facility is ultimately responsible for the lifeguard team. Yet you play a key role in helping your supervisor and leading the team. Developing the team will help you in this role and in your role as team leader.

A group of people working together is not automatically a team. *Teamwork* is a shared sense of spirit in a group of individuals. Most important, lifeguards feel part of the team and give their best for the team. Teamwork has three main benefits:

1 **The team can do its work and accomplish its goals more efficiently than a group of individuals working separately.**

2 **Individuals are better motivated to do a good job when they feel part of a team.**

3 **Everyone has more fun cooperating and working as a team.**

Team building doesn't just happen—as head lifeguard, you work to help the group act as a team. This begins with your attitude and interaction with the lifeguards: your team spirit. In addition, encourage lifeguards to talk to each other and share ideas and information. For example, urge lifeguards starting their shifts to talk to the lifeguards who are leaving to learn about any changes in the facility or anything special to watch. Establish a spirit of everyone's working together, such as when one lifeguard backs up another who is performing a rescue. Lifeguards need to feel they can trust each other for such backup and information, and you can help develop this trust by how you respond to the team.

Any activities that bring the lifeguard team together as a group also help build teamwork. In-service training and lifeguard competitions are good ways to build the team, especially if you plan ways for the lifeguards to interact socially during these activities. You can also plan purely social events for lifeguards, depending on the size of the group and the facility, to help everyone get to know each other better.

Finally, the techniques you use to motivate individuals can also help motivate and build the whole team.

Developing goals

The lifeguard team works together to accomplish common goals. You and your supervisor may develop the goals, but this process should also include the lifeguards. Start by discussing with your supervisor what each of you sees as important. You should know the overall mission of your facility or organization and communicate that mission to your lifeguard team. The goals that you, your supervisor, and the whole team develop should fit with the facility's mission. For example:

Facility's Mission: To provide opportunities and experiences contributing to the health, well-being, and development of the community through recreational activities.

Head Lifeguard's Goal: To keep the aquatic facility staffed with a trained lifeguard team to make it safe and enjoyable for the patrons.

Lifeguard Team's Goal: To score 95% or better on all unannounced evaluations for a 3-month period.

The lifeguard team's goal helps accomplish the facility's mission. Lifeguards working together to accomplish their goal realize that cooperation is needed from everyone. The group thus begins to appreciate and depend on each group member. When the group achieves its goal, members give recognition to each other naturally. The group is well on its way to becoming a team. Recognition from the facility's management also further develops team cohesiveness and motivation.

As head lifeguard, you can ensure the team's goals are developed as a team effort. Discuss the team's ideas with them. Your leadership style can help the team to agree on its goals. Everyone's ideas should be considered. Be sure all team members feel "safe" to contribute in the discussion. For example, do not let any team member make comments that inhibit the ideas of others, such as saying, "I think that's a stupid idea."

You personally will want the team to accomplish certain goals, and the team will want to set others for themselves. Whether for an individual or a group, each goal should be a *S.M.A.R.T. goal:*

- **S**—Specific (one idea, not different ideas presented together)
- **M**—Measurable (progress can be evaluated)
- **A**—Attainable (reasonably possible that the goal can be achieved)
- **R**—Relevant (compatible with the supervisor's goals and facility's mission)
- **T**—Time oriented (can be achieved within a defined period, before a proposed deadline)

Following are two examples:

Example 1

Facility goal: To improve the fitness of lifeguarding staff.

Lifeguard team goal: For each lifeguard to increase swimming ability from at least 500 yards per week at the beginning of the season to at least 1000 yards per week by the end of the season.

Example 2

Facility goal: To give cheerful customer service at entrances and exits to set a positive tone and encourage return visits.

Lifeguard team goal: When appropriate, for lifeguards not on surveillance duty to greet each patron as he or she enters and leaves the facility each day.

Once the team has agreed on goals, then you need to help your supervisor and the team accomplish them by managing the lifeguard team through its daily work. You need the following skills to do this:

- Communication
- Problem solving and decision making
- Delegation
- Motivation and recognition

These skills are discussed in the following sections.

Communication

Communication is the process of passing information or an understanding from one person to another. To manage the work of your lifeguard team, you need to communicate effectively. Again, your role is in part to bridge between the lifeguard team and your supervisor. You communicate to your supervisor the ideas of the lifeguard team about issues, concerns, procedures, or problems so that the facility management can make informed decisions and lead the team well. You also communicate to the team the decisions of your supervisor so that they clearly understand the reasons for procedures and actions they need to take.

Communication does not automatically succeed. The person may not understand your meaning as clearly and totally as you want if a barrier to effective communication is present. Barriers may come from either the speaker or the listener, or both. Speaker barriers are those factors that keep the speaking person from communicating effectively, such as the following:

- Speaking in a monotone or mumbling
- Speaking in a threatening or otherwise inappropriate tone of voice
- Using inappropriate or unfamiliar terms or vocabulary
- Not focusing on the listener or the subject—being distracted
- Using body language or facial expressions that are distracting, threatening, or inappropriate

Listener barriers are factors that keep the person from effectively hearing or understanding the message, such as the following:

- Lack of interest
- Lack of listening skills
- Distractions
- Personal feelings or attitudes about the speaker

Be aware of such barriers, and watch that they do not affect your communication as either speaker or listener. By far the most common barrier is not listening well. When someone else is expressing an opinion, our natural tendency as listeners is to begin to form our own opinion or to begin to think of a response—while the person is still talking! In other words, before someone is even finished explaining their thought, we have interpreted it. Often we are paying little attention to the person's actual message but more to how he or she says it (tone of voice) and what body language the person is using. We often concentrate more on what we are thinking than on what the other person is saying. You can see why misunderstandings so easily occur. To be an effective communicator, you need to practice conscious listening. Learn to consciously avoid the tendency to interpret, and really hear what another person has to say.

In addition to working to prevent communication barriers, practice positive communication techniques to ensure your communication is effective with both your supervisor and the lifeguards.

An important technique is to seek and use feedback about the message you are sending. Ask questions such as, "How do you understand this project?" Give feedback to others too. Repeat what you think you heard and ask, "Is that what you meant?" If you don't understand the message, ask questions to help the other person clarify the ideas. As only half of a conversation, you cannot guarantee your message will be understood perfectly, but using feedback increases the odds that others really hear what you mean to say.

Following are additional tips for effective communication:

- Learn and use the names of new lifeguards immediately. Not using a person's name can give the impression you are impersonal or cold.
- Say what you mean and mean what you say. Get right to the point instead of indirectly moving around the subject.
- Respect the feelings and ideas of the person with whom you are speaking. Work to keep the communication moving in both directions instead of you doing all the talking.
- Use specific words. Say "Please clean the deck at the end of your shift" rather than "Let's clean up this place later."
- When seeking information or ideas, ask open-ended questions rather than yes-or-no questions that limit the response of the other. For example, ask "What do you think of this?" rather than "Do you like this?"
- If the other is communicating vaguely, ask questions to help him or her focus more specifically on the topic.
- Don't be afraid to be silent. Sometimes you need to pause to give the other person time to think through his or her thoughts and find words to express them.
- Take the time to give complete information. For example, do not simply tell a new lifeguard, "Only let the swim team use the starting blocks." This communication is ineffective if the policy is to let only the swim team use the starting blocks during practice when the coach is supervising. Otherwise, the lifeguard might let anyone who says he or she is on the swim team use the blocks anytime even without supervision.

Problem solving and decision making

You usually develop *problem-solving skills* through practical experience. You can improve your skills, however, by thinking about what goes into effective problem solving. Successful problem solvers work to —

- Respect others.
- Be optimistic.
- Be willing to work hard on solutions.
- Consider creative options.
- Recognize that conflict can lead to creative solutions.

As a head lifeguard, you will use problem-solving skills. The lifeguard team will bring problems to you before going to your supervisor. If you and the team can solve these problems (Fig. 6-1), you will become even more valuable to your supervisor.

figure 6-1 *Solving problems as a group can help solidify the lifeguard team.*

You also need good decision-making skills to know which problems you should take to your supervisor rather than try to solve by yourself. Talk with your supervisor about the limits of your responsibility and when to bring problems to his or her attention. When you do need to bring a problem to your supervisor, try to present it along with one or two possible solutions. This approach shows that you have thought about the problem and are eager to help in the solution.

How you solve problems also depends on your leadership style. You can solve a problem individually if it needs an immediate solution and you have no time to consult others, such as your facility manager or your lifeguard team. Group solutions take more work to achieve, but they can solidify a lifeguard team and in most cases are worth your time.

Consider other factors involved in decision making or problem solving. Do you have authority to decide this on your own? What will be the consequences of your decision? Who is affected, and how? Is the decision consistent with facility rules and policies? What are the costs? Does it create any new problems?

In general, follow a six-step approach to solve problems:

1 Identify the problem, not the symptoms of the problem. (For example, which is the underlying problem: one child wandered off from the kiddie area or parents do not see rules posted for supervising their children?)

2 Identify all possible solutions. (Posting rules may be one solution, but having a separate lifeguard supervise the kiddie area may also be a solution.) Never assume there is only one way to solve a problem. Brainstorm with your lifeguard team for other possibilities.

3 Evaluate the alternative solutions. Which will work best? Do you have resources for it?

4 Select the solution to use. Consider whether you need approval from management to use this solution.

5 Implement the solution. Be sure to communicate clearly with everyone involved when the solution involves a change in policy or procedures.

6 Evaluate the solution. Wait long enough to give the solution a chance to work, and then determine whether the problem has been solved and no new problem has arisen. If the solution is not working as well as you had hoped, return to step 3 and reevaluate the possibilities—you may need to try an alternative solution.

Here's another example of using this process. In a community swimming pool, a scheduled learn-to-swim class is using the shallow end of the pool at the same time that a senior citizen group is performing aquatic exercise in chest-deep water. Several of the seniors say they would feel safer entering the water by the ladders in the shallow area, but the swim instructor says it would disrupt the swim class if they cross through the area. Both groups complain to the lifeguards on duty, who bring the problem to you. What are your alternatives?

- To reschedule one activity or the other even if there is room in the pool for both?
- To shift the swim class area away from one of the ladders at the shallow end, even if that cramps the class?
- To install a temporary ladder for entry at another place in the pool?

Can you think of other possible solutions? In such a case, you could brainstorm the possibilities with your lifeguards and evaluate the alternatives to choose the best solution. After you implement it, check with both groups to make sure they are satisfied with your solution.

Delegation

Delegation is entrusting others with tasks for which you are responsible. It is not getting rid of things you do not like to do because you find them boring or unpleasant. Delegation helps you multiply your efforts by dividing your duties. In other words, you can get more done in less time. The team can accomplish the goals, and everyone can share in the rewards and recognition for accomplishing them, not just the supervisor or the head lifeguard. This approach reinforces the feeling of teamwork. In addition, delegation can give individual team members the opportunity to be successful. Even if they make mistakes, they gain in their commitment to the team and can learn from the mistakes.

Delegation of a responsibility is different from assignment of a task. A lifeguard may be assigned to clean the locker room at the end of a shift, and that is the lifeguard's task. You as head lifeguard may have the responsibility to give in-service training for new lifeguards. You may delegate a part of this training to an experienced lifeguard—that is, that person helps you do your job—but that training still remains your responsibility, and you are accountable for being sure it is done well.

When you entrust duties to others, you need to follow up and give help and assistance as needed. It is still your responsibility to be sure that whatever you delegate is completed. This does not necessarily mean doing the job yourself but may mean offering additional resources to accomplish it. Regular follow up can prevent misunderstandings or major mistakes and can give you the opportunity to be an encouraging leader.

Sometimes you need to help with the task to maintain your credibility with the team. This can be especially true for maintenance duties. If you always delegate clean-up and maintenance to others, you may give the impression that you feel too important to share in all aspects of the job. Remember that as head lifeguard, you are a bridge between the team and your supervisor. You still must share in as many duties of the lifeguard team as possible to be an effective bridge.

Follow these principles for effective delegation:

- Identify the task specifically. Describe the task, and give all pertinent information and restrictions.
- Include the standards of accomplishment, and define what success means for the task. Specify the results you expect.
- Have the lifeguard restate to you what is to be done to be sure he or she understands.
- Encourage the lifeguard to make suggestions for how best to accomplish it. Motivate the lifeguard to be committed to the task.
- Let the lifeguard know how you will be monitoring the task, and provide feedback along the way.
- Hold the person accountable for completion of the task.
- If the person makes a mistake, be supportive and show him or her how you have learned from your errors.

For example, during in-service training in first aid and CPR skills you might delegate to a lifeguard who is a CPR instructor the task of evaluating the other lifeguards' CPR skills. You specify to take 30 minutes for this task, and say to check that each person performs all steps correctly. You explain to the other lifeguards why you are asking this one trained lifeguard to do the skills check. Have the lifeguard explain back to you exactly what you expect, and encourage him or her to take the initiative in organizing the other lifeguards for this skills check. Make yourself available for any questions or problems along the way and confirm that everyone's skills have been checked.

As you can see, delegation is far more than simply getting rid of responsibilities. It takes a lot of work to delegate effectively, but it's worth the effort in the development of your leadership skills and the commitment of the lifeguard team.

Motivation and recognition

Motivating staff is an important aspect of effective leadership. Even the most competent leader may find it difficult to motivate some staff members. No leader can force someone to be motivated. As a head lifeguard, you cannot make others feel as you do about job duties, nor can you force others to share your priorities. No person can control another person's feelings, attitudes, and desires. What a leader can do is create and foster an environment that inspires others to want to become motivated.

As a head lifeguard, your job includes helping facility management create a motivating environment. Feeling good about one's job is the best motivation—do anything you can think of to help your lifeguards enjoy their work. Treat them as individuals, not as workers. Be positive and courteous as you supervise them, not demanding. Praise them often for their good work. Praise reinforces positive attitudes and behavior. Praise is most effective when it immediately follows an action, when it is specific about the action (not just "You're doing a good job"), and when it is sincere. Be careful not to overdo it—your lifeguards can tell if you are sincere or not, and praise not given genuinely is not taken well.

This approach to working with your lifeguards helps them feel good about themselves as lifeguards and like their work, and that is the best way to be motivated to perform at one's best.

Praise is only one of the ways to motivate lifeguards. Recognition is another way to increase motivation. Recognizing outstanding performance lets head lifeguards and supervisors show the facility's standards and how to meet and exceed them. Recognition programs can include merit pay increases and certificates of appreciation. Many facilities and organizations have established recognition programs that you can use in your facility with your lifeguard team. Other ideas include recognition of an employee of the week, month, or year or special mention in a facility or organization newsletter or local newspaper. Employees to be recognized can be chosen by supervisors, peers, or patrons. Any recognition program should have written criteria so that everyone understands what is required to be eligible and how he or she will be judged.

Be sure you are not always recognizing the same lifeguards with whatever methods you are using. Other lifeguards may begin to feel left out and may even resent those who are recognized. This hurts the team and lowers morale. To avoid this problem, look for a variety of things to recognize. For example, if you recognize only physical skills, such as swimming ability, a lifeguard who is not among the best swimmers may never be recognized. If you also recognize abilities, such as patron contact skills, that lifeguard may be recognized and praised for particularly good work. You can also recognize improvement in any skills. Usually you can find something to recognize in everyone if you take the time to look.

Follow these guidelines for praise and recognition:

- Always let the person and others see what exactly is being praised and why it is important.
- Make the recognition more personal by showing your own appreciation for the other's good work.
- Always offer your help and support in helping the person continue to do a good job.

Other factors also increase motivation, such as team goal setting, team problem solving, and team decision making, as discussed earlier. The more the lifeguard team participates in what affects them and their jobs, the more "ownership" of their job they will feel and the more motivated they will be in their work.

Incentives are another way to help motivate people. An **incentive** is something a person wants and will act to achieve. An incentive can be an object, such as an award, or a feeling, such as knowing you did a great job and sensing others respect you for it.

Discuss incentive ideas with your supervisor and when appropriate, with the lifeguards. To choose the best incentives, you need to understand your lifeguard team. Ask others to share their ideas. Incentives may include days off, rebates on training or free training, extra uniforms, a preferred parking space, or a preferred locker location. Offer special training with a personal benefit for the individual, such as a class on interviewing techniques or resume writing. Take lifeguards out to lunch, or offer coupons for complimentary meals at local restaurants.

Incentives can be given for referring a successful candidate for employment, for returning for another season, for achieving a new higher level certification, or just for catching lifeguards "doing things right." This could include outstanding performance during an emergency, but keep in mind that many lifeguards never have an opportunity to perform in an emergency. If your facility has few rescues, that is terrific—but in that case you may have to work twice as hard to keep your lifeguards from thinking, "Nothing ever happens here." When possible, provide incentives for what your lifeguards do on a daily basis, for example, cleaning up without being asked, calming a child during minor first aid, or solving a patron's problem. Consistent praise for such everyday things will do far more to motivate your staff than traditional annual awards or recognition programs.

TEAM BUILDING

Throughout this chapter, you have learned the importance of the lifeguard team and things you can do to develop the team and motivate everyone on it to do his or her best. Much of this information comes down to one overall question: how do you as team leader interact with the lifeguards on the team? This is more than a matter of leadership style. The most effective head lifeguards are those who are closely in-volved with lifeguards and others at the facility in every possible way. A true leader cannot sit alone in a room away from those he or she is supposedly leading.

As you interact with others in your daily role as head lifeguard, use the following techniques as appropriate to help build your team and improve your leadership skills:

- *Check things out yourself.* Don't be a head lifeguard who stays in the office. Be visible. Get out and work with your staff often (Fig. 6-2). Observe your facility and lifeguard team in operation.
- *Have regular meetings.* Do not underestimate the power of communicating often. Your lifeguard team needs the benefit of your knowledge and experience, and you need their ideas and observations. Meetings are a great forum for sharing this information.
- *Participate in social events, such as barbecues and staff parties.* This is a good time to develop a stronger relationship and motivate your team. You can also use this time to elicit feedback from your lifeguard team, who will be more relaxed in a social atmosphere and may be more willing to share any problems they perceive.
- *Elicit public feedback.* This feedback can alert you and your supervisor to problems that can be cor-rected while they remain relatively minor. Your pa-trons are usually willing to share with you how they feel about the facility (Fig. 6-3). You and your super-visor can do this both informally, by getting out and talking with patrons, as well as formally by survey-ing patrons to determine their satisfaction with your programs, services, and staff.
- *Have lifeguards evaluate you.* Supervisors should be regularly evaluated. You can gain insight into how your team views you as a leader if you have team members fill out an anonymous evaluation that as-sesses your leadership qualities and effectiveness. Be prepared that not all comments will be constructive, although many can be very helpful as you work to maintain or improve your relationship with the mem-bers of your lifeguard team.
- *Personally conduct new employee orientations.* Orientations are discussed in Chapter 5. These orien-tations can give you information about new life-guards and are your first opportunity to start motivat-ing the team. If you are responsible for a portion of the orientation, be sure to give all the information the new lifeguards need and use your communication skills to ensure that everyone understands.

figure 6-2 *Working with your staff helps build the life-guard team and improve your own leadership skills.*

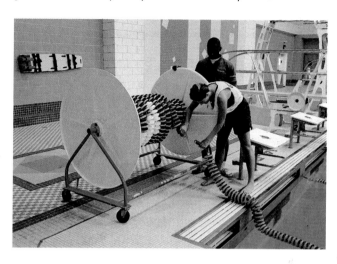

figure 6-3 *Feedback from patrons can alert you to poten-tial problems with patron satisfaction.*

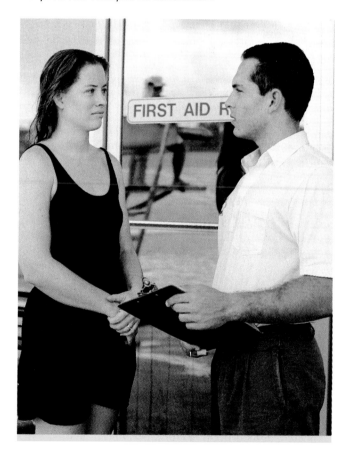

- *Be available and approachable*. Talk with your staff. Try not to make them wait to speak to you. If you are on the telephone or speaking with a customer, it is common courtesy to acknowledge someone who has come to see you and indicate you will be with him or her in a moment. Availability also means being present as much as possible. Your staff will acknowledge a problem more easily if you are standing there than if they have to make an appointment to speak with you about it later.

SUPERVISING THE LIFEGUARD TEAM

As the leader of the lifeguard team, your role is also supervisory. This may involve two additional responsibilities: helping individual lifeguards improve their performance when you note a problem behavior and conducting periodic performance evaluations.

Improving performance

Sometimes you may observe and need to correct problem behavior of a lifeguard. A lifeguard may be frequently late to report for a shift or talking to friends while on surveillance. As supervisor of the team, you need to help the lifeguard correct this problem and improve his or her behavior.

Follow certain principles when correcting problem behavior. When you see or learn of a problem behavior, follow these principles to resolve the problem positively.

- Don't approach the problem behavior from a confrontational standpoint.
- When dealing with a lifeguard on any issue, address the situation, the problem, or the behavior, not the person. Discuss the matter privately, if possible. Don't let your correction become a personal matter between you and the lifeguard.
- Keep a positive relationship with your employees. Be honest and sincere, and show respect for the person.

Your lifeguards are entitled to feedback, both positive and corrective. If a lifeguard is not measuring up to the expected, agreed-upon *performance level,* he or she has

a right to know it. Meet with the person as soon as possible, such as after the lifeguard's shift.

Prepare for this meeting so that you can present a clear understanding of the nature of the problem. Relate the problem to specific job functions or facility policies or rules. Consider the lifeguard's training and orientation to ensure that the lifeguard knows the specific job functions, policies, and rules. Be ready to explain to the lifeguard the actual or potential impact of the problem behavior, such as ineffective surveillance that could lead to not spotting a distressed swimmer quickly. Consider whether factors outside the lifeguard's control may be contributing to the problem, such as harassment by patrons or incompatibility with other peers. Be prepared to offer constructive solutions and give clear performance expectations. Remain open to additional or different solutions the lifeguard may offer, but go to the meeting with a definite outcome you expect. Remember not to attack the individual. Focus on the behavior.

When correcting a lifeguard, take the time to describe what you have observed. Point out the negative effect of the problem behavior. Always allow the lifeguard the chance to respond to your comments. Offer specific suggestions and solutions, and ask for the lifeguard's input on the suggested solutions to the problem. Make sure the lifeguard understands what actions and results you expect to see, and agree on a specific date for reviewing the situation. End this meeting with a summary of what you have agreed upon and a sincere offer of your support.

If the problem behavior still occurs after the correction date, talk with your supervisor about what further corrective actions are needed.

Evaluation

Performance evaluation is a constructive process to determine how well all lifeguards are performing. This process acknowledges lifeguards' current effective performance and helps them improve in the future. As a head lifeguard, you may participate in or provide input for lifeguard evaluations. Evaluation is not a disciplinary procedure. It is a review of a lifeguard's overall performance over a period of time. Evaluation should recognize what the lifeguard does well and assess what improvement is needed.

The lifeguard should not be surprised by the evaluation. Since the evaluation is a review, it naturally includes performance items the lifeguard already knows about and items you have already discussed with him or her. Don't wait until the evaluation is due before considering what to put in a lifeguard's evaluation. Make evaluation an on-going, daily process. If you see a problem that requires immediate attention, such as behavior that impedes the lifeguard's surveillance and thus may affect patrons' safety, correct it immediately—don't wait for the next performance evaluation.

As head lifeguard, you usually have the opportunity for daily evaluation, and therefore your supervisor often needs your assistance in the formal performance evaluations in the facility.

Evaluations and correction are based on a set of standards and expectations for the job. These standards should be included in the facility's policies and procedures manual for employees. Standards and expectations should include the job description, as well as a detailed description of what the lifeguard is accountable for. For example, standards may state the lifeguard's responsibilities for the following:

- Actions in emergency situations, first aid procedures, and zone and rotation procedures
- Reporting absences and filling out time records
- Opening and closing procedures

These standards may be developed in conjunction with the lifeguard team. If team members help set their own standards, they are more likely to support those standards.

figure 6-4 *An example of a lifeguard evaluation form.*

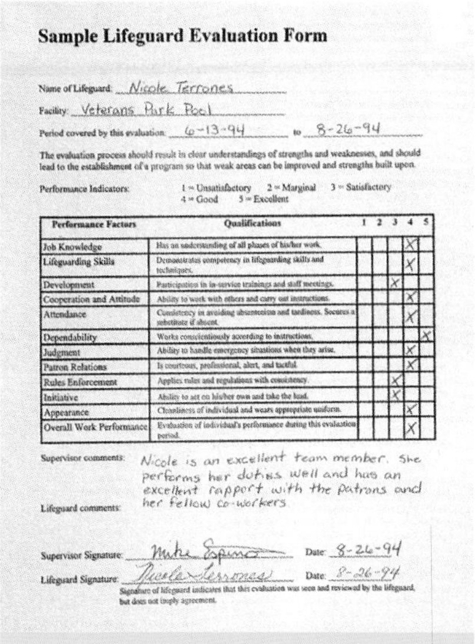

Sample Lifeguard Evaluation Form

Name of Lifeguard: Nicole Terrones

Facility: Veterans Park Pool

Period covered by this evaluation: 6-13-94 to 8-26-94

The evaluation process should result in clear understandings of strengths and weaknesses, and should lead to the establishment of a program so that weak areas can be improved and strengths built upon.

Performance Indicators: 1 = Unsatisfactory 2 = Marginal 3 = Satisfactory 4 = Good 5 = Excellent

Performance Factors	Qualifications	1	2	3	4	5
Job Knowledge	Has an understanding of all phases of his/her work.				X	
Lifeguarding Skills	Demonstrates competency in lifeguarding skills and techniques.				X	
Development	Participation in in-service trainings and staff meetings.			X		
Cooperation and Attitude	Ability to work with others and carry out instructions.				X	
Attendance	Consistency in avoiding absenteeism and tardiness. Secures a substitute if absent.				X	
Dependability	Works conscientiously according to instructions.					X
Judgment	Ability to handle emergency situations when they arise.				X	
Patron Relations	Is courteous, professional, alert, and tactful.				X	
Rules Enforcement	Applies rules and regulations with consistency.			X		
Initiative	Ability to act on his/her own and take the lead.			X		
Appearance	Cleanliness of individual and wears appropriate uniform.				X	
Overall Work Performance	Evaluation of individual's performance during this evaluation period.				X	

Supervisor comments: Nicole is an excellent team member. She performs her duties well and has an excellent rapport with the patrons and her fellow co-workers

Lifeguard comments:

Supervisor Signature: Mike Espinoza Date: 8-26-94

Lifeguard Signature: Nicole Terrones Date: 8-26-94

Signature of lifeguard indicates that this evaluation was seen and reviewed by the lifeguard, but does not imply agreement.

The lifeguard evaluation form

A ***lifeguard evaluation form*** is used to document a lifeguard's job performance (Fig. 6-4). This form should be included in the facility's policies and procedures manual. It should be specific enough to inform the lifeguard what job performance is expected. Review the form with each lifeguard when completed. Forward copies of the evaluation form to proper offices, such as the facility manager or personnel department. Keep a copy at the facility, and give lifeguards their own copy. See Appendix J for a sample evaluation form.

Lifeguards are evaluated on the basis of specific criteria, such as the following:

- Job knowledge of all responsibilities
- Lifeguarding skills: swimming ability, rescue skills, first aid, and CPR
- Development: participation in in-service training sessions
- Cooperation and attitude: ability to work with the head lifeguard, facility management, and other staff members and accept responsibility and authority
- Attendance: prompt to report to work
- Dependability
- Judgment: ability to decide how to act in emergencies
- Patron relationships
- Rules enforcement
- Initiative: able to act on own as needed
- Appearance: cleanliness and proper uniform

A number of different methods are in use for evaluating lifeguards. Some head lifeguards or facility managers use a numerical scale (1 = low, 5 = high). Another method is to give a rating of poor, average, superior, or excellent. A third method combines these, giving each performance factor a point grade, such as 1 = "does not perform," 2 = "performs to minimum standards," and 3 = "performs above minimum standards." The points on the different criteria are then totaled. An aquatic facility can adapt any of these methods. Whatever method you use, be sure it is used in a standardized way for all lifeguards.

Ideally, the lifeguards on your team will have good evaluations or will be able to correct weak areas quickly. The facility usually has policies and procedures for actions to take if a lifeguard has a poor evaluation and is unwilling or unable to improve. Your supervisor is responsible for any disciplinary actions needed.

SUMMARY

As leader of the lifeguard team, you have many responsibilities. Developing a spirit of teamwork and cooperation helps your team meet its goals. Your leadership and communication skills also help you solve problems that may occur and help motivate the lifeguards on your team. As their immediate supervisor, you help them correct any problems in their performance and assist management in their performance evaluations.

STUDY QUESTIONS

Circle the letter of the best answer or answers.

1. The head lifeguard represents the lifeguards to management and management to the lifeguards. In order to communicate well with both groups, the head lifeguard's goal should be to—
   a) Support the lifeguards in all instances.
   b) Support management in all instances.
   c) Support management while maintaining the trust and confidence of the lifeguards.
   d) Support management if you know your lifeguards will agree.

2. Which of the following are the main benefits of teamwork?
   a) Individuals working separately are better motivated to do a good job.
   b) The team can do its work and accomplish its goals more efficiently than a group of individuals working separately.
   c) Everyone has more fun cooperating and working as a team.
   d) Individuals are better motivated to do a good job when they feel like part of a team.

3. Which of the following benefits can be attributed to lifeguards working together to accomplish their goal?
   a) Increased cooperation.
   b) Increased appreciation of the group members.
   c) Increased cohesiveness and motivation.
   d) Individual success.

4. Which of the following tips can lead to more effective communication between the head lifeguard and the lifeguard team?
   a) Learn and use the names of new lifeguards immediately.
   b) Only yell when absolutely necessary.
   c) Use specific words.
   d) Say what you mean and mean what you say.
   e) Respect the feelings and ideas of the person with whom you are speaking.
   f) Ask yes-or-no questions that limit the response of the other person.
5. Which of the following is not a good way to motivate members of a lifeguard team?
   a) Treat them as individuals, not as workers.
   b) Be positive and courteous as you supervise them, not demanding.
   c) Point out mistakes quickly, so they can improve their performance.
   d) Praise effective work often.
6. Which of the following techniques can help build a lifeguard team and improve your leadership skills?
   a) Stay in the office as much as possible.
   b) Have regular meetings.
   c) Participate in social events.
   d) Be sure lifeguards make an appointment to speak with you.
   e) Have the lifeguards evaluate you.
   f) Personally conduct new employee orientations.

7. Which of the following criteria are appropriate for evaluating a lifeguard?
   a) Knowledge of all job responsibilities
   b) Lifeguarding skills
   c) Judgment: the ability to decide how to act in an emergency
   d) Initiative: the ability to act on his or her own as needed
8. List the six steps for effective problem solving in their correct order.
   ___ Identify all possible solutions.
   ___ Evaluate the solution.
   ___ Implement the solution.
   ___ Identify the problem.
   ___ Select the solution to use.
   ___ Evaluate the alternative solutions.

Circle *True* or *False*.
9. Delegating a responsibility is the same as assigning a task. True or False?
10. When correcting a lifeguard's problem behavior, remember to focus on the individual, not on the behavior itself. True or False?

See answers to study questions on p. 121.

Objectives

After reading this chapter, you should be able to—

1. List and explain at least five general guidelines for developing a positive relationship with patrons.
2. Explain at least five general principles that apply when dealing with problem situations.
3. Explain the five-step approach to resolve conflict.
4. Describe at least five conflict management strategies.
5. Explain how a head lifeguard deals with violence at an aquatic facility.
6. Explain how a head lifeguard deals with a problem situation involving more than one person (groups).
7. Explain why one must look beyond cultural differences when supervising patrons.
8. List four guidelines for working with patrons who do not speak English.
9. List two aspects of cultural behavior relevant to lifeguarding situations.
10. Describe three general categories of disabilities.
11. Explain the different ways to communicate with disabled patrons.
12. Define the key terms for this chapter.

Key Terms

Accommodations: Arrangements to help people with disabilities participate in programs and activities.

Cultural diversity: Differences among groups of people related to cultural background and exemplified through customs, beliefs, and practices.

Disability: The loss, absence, or impairment of motor, sensory, or mental function.

Hearing impairment: Partial or total loss of hearing.

Mainstreaming: Including people with disabilities in the same programs and activities as the non-disabled.

Sensory function: The ability to see, hear, sense, touch, and taste.

Tactile impairment: Partial or total loss of the sense of touch.

Vision impairment: Partial or total loss of sight.

INTRODUCTION

As a head lifeguard, you lead the lifeguard team at your facility. The team's responsibilities involve interacting with patrons. Therefore you and your lifeguards need good public relations skills. As head lifeguard, you are both an important contact for the patrons who visit your facility and a role model for the lifeguards you supervise. All facility management have the general goals of keeping patrons safe and helping patrons enjoy themselves while in the facility. In some facilities, the lifeguards may also have an explicit customer service role to ensure patrons are satisfied with their experience.

Effective communication with the public is one of the **cornerstones** of lifeguarding. The lifeguards on your team must know when and how they should communicate with patrons. Although lifeguards are often in direct contact with patrons, at times they cannot interrupt what they are doing to talk with patrons or resolve conflicts. For example, a lifeguard on surveillance duty cannot compromise safety by dealing with questions, suggestions, or problems for more than a few seconds. In these situations you, not the lifeguard, have the key interaction with patrons. The lifeguards on your team need to know their exact role in patron relations and when to call you for help.

Interacting with the public can be rewarding and challenging. Even if you usually encounter cooperative, friendly patrons, you must also be prepared to deal with patrons who are uncooperative or even violent. You may also interact with members of various cultural groups and patrons with disabilities. This chapter focuses on skills and strategies you can use to interact with all patrons in various situations.

INTERACTING POSITIVELY WITH THE PUBLIC

Any time you are interacting with the public, your actions should promote an atmosphere of trust and goodwill. The following general guidelines help develop a positive relationship with patrons:

figure 7-1 *Make every patron feel welcome, important, and respected.*

- *Treat people as you would like to be treated.* Make every patron feel welcome, important, and respected (Fig. 7-1).
- *Be professional at all times.* Conduct yourself in a courteous, mature, and responsible way. Never insult or argue with a patron.
- *Avoid unnecessary conversation with other employees or patrons while on duty.*
- *When interacting with patrons, speak clearly and make direct eye contact.* (Remove your sunglasses if necessary.)
- *Take all suggestions and complaints seriously, and follow up as necessary.* Avoid blaming anyone. Direct complaints you cannot handle to the pool manager, facility operator, or other staff; follow your facility's procedures.
- *Do not make promises you cannot keep.*
- *Keep interactions brief and direct.* Direct patrons who need more information to the appropriate staff.
- *Enforce rules fairly and consistently.* Be positive and nonjudgmental. Reinforce correct behavior.
- *Take a sincere interest in all patrons.*

All patrons visiting your facility expect a safe and enjoyable experience. As head lifeguard, you help establish and maintain a positive environment. Use in-service training to help prepare your lifeguards for a cooperative relationship with patrons. Your facility's policies for interaction with patrons can also contribute to a positive relationship between lifeguarding staff and patrons.

Facility policies for interaction

Every facility has specific guidelines for interacting with patrons. You must be completely familiar with the policies and guidelines at your facility. Communicate these guidelines to your lifeguard team through your words and actions. For example, you can demonstrate how to enforce rules and correct problem behaviors without offending patrons. When lifeguards understand what is expected of them, they are better able to interact with patrons appropriately.

The facility's policies and procedures manual may have a section on public relations. Review this material with the lifeguards from time to time. If the manual does not include this information, talk with your supervisor about adding it.

figure 7-2 *Problem behaviors occur when a patron breaks a rule or behaves in a way that needs to be corrected.*

figure 7-3 *Rules should be posted where patrons can see them.*

PROBLEM BEHAVIOR

Ideally, all interactions with the public would be positive, but unfortunately, problems do occur. In general, you and your lifeguards may face two kinds of situations that require special skills for interacting with patrons. Problem behaviors occur when a patron who is generally cooperative breaks a rule or behaves in a way that needs to be corrected for his or her safety or that of others. For example, a child simply gets excited and starts running on the deck—not to rebel or intentionally cause trouble, but just in the emotion of the moment (Fig. 7-2).

A different kind of situation occurs when uncooperative patrons, who, for whatever reason, intentionally break rules and do not cooperate with your attempts to correct the problem.

Preventing problems

The best approach to problem behavior is to prevent problems before they occur. This does not happen automatically. Achieving the respect of patrons and encouraging their responsible behavior take time and effort to develop. You and your lifeguard team can positively influence the behavior of patrons in three general ways:

- *Appearance and Behavior:* Dress and behave professionally at all times. Patrons have more respect for staff members who look neat and organized and treat others with courtesy and respect.
- *Posting Rules:* When you list and explain rules and expectations in advance, you make it easier for patrons to behave correctly. Post rules where patrons can see them (Fig. 7-3). Make sure they can be understood by all patrons.
- *Enforcement:* Enforce policies, rules, and regulations fairly and consistently. Inconsistent enforcement can confuse and frustrate patrons and lead to problem behaviors and possibly unsafe situations. Lifeguards should also obey all the rules they enforce.

---

figure 7-4 *Do not overreact while handling a problem situation.*

Responding to problems

Regardless of what you and your facility do to prevent problem behavior, it may occur at times. Following are general principles for dealing with such situations.

1. *Anticipate Problems:* You can avoid many potential problems by staying one step ahead of a situation. Be alert to signs that indicate a problem is beginning, and try to defuse the situation before the problem erupts. For example, if you see two or three teenagers starting to have a loud argument, you might try to intervene early instead of waiting to see if the argument leads to a fist fight. Don't let small incidents "snowball" into big problems.

2. *Do Not Overreact:* Acting as if every incident is a crisis can create more problems and make you less effective as a leader (Fig. 7-4).

3. *Focus on the Behavior, Not the Individual:* Correct a patron's specific behavior without criticizing or ridiculing the person. For example, you might say "Running on the deck isn't safe" rather than "*You* shouldn't be running on the deck."

4. *Respect Patrons' Feelings:* Always respect a patron's feelings when correcting a behavior. Treat that person as you would like to be treated. Avoid embarrassing anyone in front of his or her peers.

5. *Be Firm, Fair, and Friendly:* Approach all situations in a positive, professional manner. A helpful attitude is particularly effective in situations that involve problem behavior.

6. *Don't Pretend to Know it All:* Keep an open mind as you interact with patrons. Patrons rarely defy facility rules and procedures deliberately. Give everyone the benefit of the doubt. For example, first assume the person doesn't understand the rule rather than assuming the person is deliberately breaking it.

7. *Use Suspension as a Last Resort:* Think twice before asking a patron to leave the facility. Do so only after exhausting every available alternative. Be sure to follow facility policy for asking a person to leave.

Responding appropriately to problem behavior can at times be difficult. These seven guidelines are general ways to address such situations, and you can also use methods you learn from your experience. Be sure to follow your facility's specific policies and procedures.

The more experience you have interacting with the public, the more comfortable and effective you will become in problem situations. How you react in a situation also depends on whether the patron involved is uncooperative or potentially violent.

UNCOOPERATIVE PATRONS

Most patrons willingly follow rules and procedures. However, no matter how fair and consistent you and your lifeguard team are when enforcing rules, you may occasionally encounter an uncooperative patron. As a head lifeguard, your responsibility may include intervening when a lifeguard cannot get a patron to cooperate. Make sure that your lifeguards know to contact you if a conflict occurs. Talk to your supervisor about the facility's policy in such cases. The responsibility for dealing with uncooperative patrons may belong either to you or another member of management.

An uncooperative patron is one who, after you or a lifeguard has tried to motivate the person to follow the rules, deliberately persists in problem behavior. Uncooperative behavior may occur for a variety of reasons: a patron may be under the influence of alcohol or other drugs, a conflict between two or more patrons may lead to disruptive or unsafe behavior, or a patron may simply feel like causing trouble. Regardless of the cause of the uncooperative behavior, you must act right away, since patrons who break the rules endanger themselves and others.

In any situation, start by being courteous and attempting to interact positively while maintaining safety. Before you or another lifeguard assumes a patron is uncooperative, make sure he or she understands the rules. Communication barriers may result from many situations, including a disability or a difference in language. If you discover a language barrier, be patient, assess the situation, and try to ease it with the communication **strategies** presented in Chapter 6 and later in this chapter.

Conflict resolution

Uncooperative behavior may **escalate** into conflict. A conflict may occur between two or more patrons or between a patron and a staff person or a lifeguard who is not on surveillance duty. The general principles are the same in all cases. You use intervention strategies to resolve conflicts between patrons and between lifeguards and patrons. Follow these general principles, if possible, when attempting to resolve a conflict with an uncooperative person:

- Plan ahead before intervening in the conflict.
- Follow the policies and procedures in the facility's manual.
- Use the steps for conflict resolution described below.
- If you are having difficulty handling a situation, pass the problem up the chain of command.

Use the five-step approach below to resolve conflict:

1 *Cool Off:* Regardless of whether you are resolving the conflict of others or are in conflict yourself with another person, a cooling-off period is needed. Emotions are running high, and everyone involved needs time to cool down. You also need time to carefully "read" or assess the feelings of those involved before attempting to work through conflict. Wait until those involved are feeling calm enough to talk about the problem.

2 *State the Problem:* Everyone needs the opportunity to express his or her feelings. Ask the person to give his or her version of the problem. Don't let the other person speak until the first finishes with steps 3 and 4; then ask the other to give his or her version and repeat this process.

3 *State the Feeling:* Encourage the first person to state what he or she feels about the problem. Encourage the person to be specific. For example, "I'm angry because this guy jumped on me in the water."

4 *State What You Want:* Be sure the first person states what he or she wants to happen. For example, "I want him to apologize and keep away from me in the water."

5 *Resolve the Conflict:* After hearing both sides, you need to decide whether they are ready to resolve the situation. If you think one person is still being uncooperative, you may want to drop the issue and separate the two, making sure they stay away from each other. If both have calmed down and seem open to a solution, you can use one of the following conflict management strategies:

- *Separating:* Separate the individuals if resolution seems unlikely.
- *Apologizing:* Have both people apologize without either having to accept blame.
- *Avoiding:* Encourage one person to decide it's not worth the bother and to "give in" to the other person's position.
- *Chance:* Choose a technique, such as flipping a coin, to settle a conflict.
- *Compromising:* Encourage both people to agree to give up something to resolve the conflict.
- *Humor:* Diffuse the tension by making light of the situation in a way that does not anger or offend those involved.
- *Postponing:* Agree to wait for a better time to handle the conflict.
- *Seeking Help:* Seek consultation or help when your efforts have failed.
- *Sharing:* Help both agree to share responsibility in resolving the situation.

Dealing with violence

A conflict may lead to violence if it is not resolved. As a head lifeguard, you may be the first to act in situations that are about to or have already become violent. Following all guidelines described so far in this chapter, such as reinforcing positive behavior and enforcing rules fairly, helps reduce the possibility of violence. Yet there are times when violence erupts suddenly. Violent acts can include fist fights, assaults, pushing, threats with weapons of any sort, aggressive taunting, **molestation,** rape, and drive-by shootings.

Your facility should have policies and procedures for dealing with violent acts—whether they occur in or outside the facility. There should be an emergency action plan for every potential situation. If your facility's manual lacks plans for such situations, speak to your supervisor about adding them. Don't wait until a violent situation occurs before you decide how to deal with it. You may ask local law enforcement for assistance in developing facility procedures for violent incidents. Most important, all staff members should know and practice the procedures. In violent situations, action must be prompt, decisive, and appropriate to convey the clear message: disrespect for rules and violation of laws will not be tolerated.

Follow these basic guidelines in violent situations:

- *Call immediately for assistance as outlined in your emergency action plan.* Don't hesitate to call even if you only suspect that something is about to happen.
- *In some situations, areas of the facility may need to be cleared of people.* Implement your emergency action plan for clearing an area, and start crowd control procedures. To keep all patrons safe, it may be necessary to evacuate the entire facility or provide shelter within the facility.
- *Stay at least 6 feet away from a violent person.* Stand at an angle to a violent person, rather than squarely facing him or her (Fig. 7-5). This allows you a better escape if the person kicks or punches.
- *Approaching with one or more staff members may be safer than a one-on-one confrontation with a patron.*
- *Assess the situation before intervening.* Consider the size and temperament of the people involved, the level of hostility in the situation, and your size and physical capabilities, as well as those of the patrons and your staff.
- *If weapons are involved, immediately evacuate patrons from the area or provide cover within the facility.* Do not approach an individual who has a weapon. Call the police immediately.

figure 7-5 *For your safety, stand at a distance when dealing with a violent person.*

Knowing how and when to intervene in a potentially violent situation is a complex matter. Talk with your supervisor about contacting your local police department for guidance on preventing violence at your facility and what to do if it erupts. (For further information about dealing with violence, see Chapter 2 in *American Red Cross Lifeguarding Today*.)

Problems with groups

The preceding sections on uncooperative patrons and violence discuss how to handle these problems with one or two individuals. At times, however, you may have to deal with a problem situation involving a group. For example, gang activity is causing more disruptive or violent confrontations at aquatic facilities nationwide.

In addition to the strategies described already, follow these guidelines when interacting with troublesome groups:

- Offer a friendly, accepting environment at your facility.
- Be sure the group knows the rules and regulations to be enforced; treat all patrons fairly and consistently.
- Treat the group, and each member, with respect.
- Treat each member as an individual.
- Learn their language; understand their language and idioms.
- Never "call one down" in front of his or her group. Make sure that no member loses face with his or her peers.
- Don't back a group or individual into a corner without giving the group or the person an honorable way out.
- Be willing to listen.
- Make them feel responsible for reaching a positive outcome.

CULTURAL DIVERSITY

The word "culture" refers to life patterns within a community group. ***Cultural diversity*** can involve behavior or traits related to age, gender, race, ethnicity, religion, sexual orientation, **socioeconomic** conditions, and other factors.

Patrons at your aquatic facility may come from many diverse cultures (Fig. 7-6, *A-D*). You may see cultural differences related to customs, beliefs, and behaviors.

figure 7-6 *A-D, Patrons at your aquatic facility may come from diverse cultures.*

A

B

C

D

You and your lifeguards need to be sensitive to your cultural heritages and to the varied backgrounds of the patrons with whom you interact. You should become familiar with the diverse cultures of people who use your facility.

As a head lifeguard, your job includes developing a climate in your facility that accepts differences, respects and values others, and encourages the human dignity of all. You must demonstrate patience, understanding, and flexibility.

You may want to develop in-service training programs to educate lifeguards about the cultural groups that use your facility. The more lifeguards and other staff understand about cultural differences, the more comfortable they will be interacting with patrons of different backgrounds. You can ask the local Red Cross unit to refer you to activities or courses in your community that increase awareness of cultural beliefs and practices. "Serving the Diverse Community," offered by some American Red Cross units, is one such course.

Although cultural differences may lead to differences in patrons' appearance and behavior, culture is irrelevant when a person is drowning. Remember that a drowning person shows instinctive, universal behaviors. Emphasize to lifeguards to look for these specific behaviors and not conduct surveillance according to a patron's personal or cultural characteristics.

While cultural factors are not related to the risk of drowning, they may lead to other differences, such as dress. Cultures have different standards for appropriate clothing in various situations. Patrons from one cultural background may prefer to swim in more or less clothing than someone from a different background. For example, a patron may wear a turban or headpiece at all times. If a patron's attire conflicts with your facility's swimming attire policy, be as flexible as possible when considering a request for an exception to a rule about swimming attire. Safety and facility policies should be factors in your decision. If you cannot accommodate a patron's request, explain to the patron why specific rules and regulations are in the best interest of safety. The facility's policies and procedures manual should include specific guidelines for issues such as swimming attire.

Language is another area affected by cultural background. Some patrons may not know enough English to read or understand facility rules posted only in English. If your area has a large population of one or more ethnic groups with limited knowledge of English, signs should be posted also in the language of those groups (Fig. 7-7). Signs with pictures or symbols are also helpful. Use translated signs and signs with pictures or symbols for pool rules and regulations, depth markings, and warning signs (Fig. 7-8). Depth markings should be posted in meters as well as in feet.

figure 7-7 *Bilingual signs are useful if your area has one or more ethnic groups with limited knowledge of English.*

figure 7-8 *Signs with universal pictures and symbols help relay rules and regulations.*

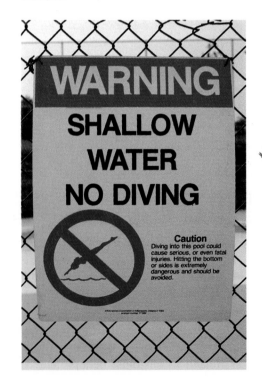

Follow these guidelines when interacting with patrons who do not speak English:

- Use your attire to let a patron know you are a lifeguard. This prepares the person for your message.
- Try to communicate in English first. Speak slowly and clearly. Do not shout. The patron may know some words and phrases in English.
- If the patron does not understand you in English, try another language if you know one.
- If you have no language in common with the patron, see if another person there can interpret for you.

You may also talk with the facility's management about employing staff who speak languages in addition to English.

As a head lifeguard, you may be faced with a variety of circumstances relating to cultural diversity. Understanding the populations using your facility will help you develop appropriate policies and procedures. You have a key role in helping your lifeguard team interact with culturally diverse patrons. A culturally aware head lifeguard is an asset to any facility.

PATRONS WITH DISABILITIES

In your interaction with all patrons at a facility, you may interact with patrons who have different disabilities. A loss, absence, or impairment of sensory, mental, or motor function is called a *disability.* In recent years, facilities have increasingly included people with disabilities in the same programs and activities as the non-disabled, a process called *mainstreaming.* This means individuals with a variety of disabilities may use your aquatic facility (Fig. 7-9). As a head lifeguard, you must make sure that patrons who have disabilities have the same safe and enjoyable experience as other patrons.

The Americans With Disabilities Act (ADA) ensures that people with disabilities have access to a wide range of opportunities and services. Making aquatic facilities safer and more accessible for people with disabilities may require your facility to make special arrangements, or *accommodations.* Accommodations may include changes in the facility's policies, procedures, programs, or physical features. You and your lifeguards should understand how the ADA affects your facility and its services.

You may or may not be able to identify patrons with disabilities. Some patrons tell lifeguards of their condition; others do not.

When working with patrons with disabilities and training your staff to work with them, remember that you cannot assume any two people are alike. Some disabilities may affect a patron's ability to participate in aquatic activities; others may not. Even two people with the same disability may have completely different abilities. Some patrons with disabilities may need assistance and accommodations; others may not. You and your lifeguard team should provide assistance only as requested. Do not base the supervision you give to disabled patrons on their physical or mental characteristics alone.

Another consideration is communication. Some people with disabilities have difficulty reading or understanding rules and regulations. You can develop and implement policies and procedures to accommodate such patrons. Strategies to improve communication with patrons with disabilities are discussed later in this chapter.

The following sections describe three general categories of disabilities: *sensory function,* **mental function,** and **motor function.** (Chapter 2 of *Lifeguarding Today* provides detailed information on these categories.) Patrons may be disabled in one or more of these areas.

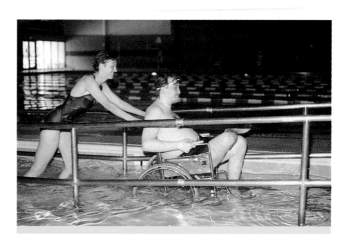

figure 7-9 *Individuals with a variety of disabilities may use your facility.*

Sensory function

Sensory function includes the ability to hear, see, smell, touch, and taste. An impairment in any of these senses may cause communication difficulties, balance problems, or inability to sense touch and pain. Sensory impairments can affect a person's safety in and around the water, how he or she behaves in and around the water, and how he or she communicates. A person with one sense impaired may compensate by using other senses more.

Hearing impairment. *Hearing impairment* is a partial or total loss of hearing. People with hearing impairments rely more on visual communication. Some may also have trouble with balance or coordination, which may require them to adapt how they swim or walk.

Following are some strategies for accommodating and communicating with patrons with hearing impairments:

- Get the patron's attention before you speak to him or her by gently tapping on the patron's shoulder or waving your hand where he or she can see it. You may have to ask someone else to help you make contact with a hearing-impaired patron, especially if you are trying to enforce a rule from a distance.
- Maintain eye contact.
- Be especially calm and patient.
- Determine if the patron can read lips. Even if he or she can, the patron may understand only 30 to 40 percent of what you say (or even less). Lip-reading is more difficult for the patron if the person to whom he or she is talking has a foreign accent or a beard or mustache.
- Face the patron while you are speaking to him or her. Keep your head level so that the person can see your mouth.
- Speak clearly and distinctly. Even if you determine that the patron cannot read lips, speak as you gesture or use signs. Don't exaggerate the volume or speed of your speech unless the patron asks you to.
- Do not shout; if the patron has even partial hearing and is wearing a hearing aid, shouting could distort his or her hearing.
- Try **pantomiming,** using broad gestures.
- Use written messages, but keep them simple.
- If possible and acceptable to the person, use an interpreter who can communicate in sign language.

Vision impairment. *Vision impairment* is a partial or total loss of sight. A person with a vision impairment may have difficulty reading signs and markings, identifying lifeguards, and seeing changes in elevation, such as steps. He or she may compensate with greater use of hearing and touch.

When interacting with a patron with a vision impairment, follow these guidelines:

- Determine if the patron also has a hearing impairment.
- Do not shout.
- When giving directions, explain things in detail.
- If a patron seems to need assistance, offer your help but do not give it unless the offer is accepted.
- If the patron accepts your offer of assistance, ask if he or she would like to take your arm. If so, brush your forearm against the patron's so that he or she can grip your arm above the elbow.
- If the patron can walk and needs to be led, lead him or her by positioning yourself one step ahead and one step to the side, letting the patron rest his or her hand at the inside of your bent elbow. Walk forward slowly, alerting the patron to any obstacles.
- Identify the source of any strange noises.

Tactile impairment. *Tactile impairment* is a partial or total loss of the sense of touch. A lack of sensation should not keep anyone out of the water. However, since people with tactile impairment may not feel scratches, abrasions, or burns, they must take special care to avoid excessive exposure to the sun and scraping their skin in the pool and on the deck. Patrons with tactile impairments may need to wear protective footwear or clothing into the water.

Mental function

Mental function refers to the brain's capacity to reason and process information. People with mental function impairments may learn more slowly than others and have trouble understanding and remembering rules. This does not mean they are being difficult or uncooperative.

Most individuals with impairments in intelligence or information processing can participate in regular aquatic programs and activities. Some patrons may have trouble following directions and safety procedures, interacting with others, or dealing with reality. Some patrons may appear confused or disoriented. They may require additional surveillance or close attention from instructors or aides. As head lifeguard, be sure your lifeguard team knows to contact you for additional assistance with coverage or communication. In most circumstances when a patron who has a mental impairment uses an aquatic facility, an aide or counselor accompanies and supervises him or her. The aide or counselor can assist you and other lifeguards with communication as necessary.

When communicating with patrons with a mental impairment, such as Down syndrome, follow these guidelines:

- Determine the patron's level of understanding by asking questions, or ask the parent, aide, or friend of the individual about the person's abilities.
- Speak slowly and distinctly, and use words and terms the patron is likely to understand.
- Listen carefully. Wait for a delayed response when it is the patron's turn to answer or respond; have patience.
- Evaluate the patron's understanding by asking a few questions, and reexplain something if necessary.
- Keep explanations short and simple.

When interacting with patrons with mental impairments, you and your lifeguard team should be aware that such patrons may also have limited motor function and balance. Nonetheless, they are still more like than unlike their non-disabled peers.

Motor function

Motor function involves many physical processes by which the brain controls the muscles for activity. A person may have limited or no ability to use one or more body parts if motor function is impaired.

Motor function can be impaired by many conditions, including **paralysis, cerebral palsy, muscular dystrophy, multiple sclerosis,** or loss of a limb. Although people with motor impairments may have problems with balance and a restricted range of joint motion, they can often move well in the water. Swimming can be an important recreational and **therapeutic** activity.

Individuals with missing or nonfunctioning limbs may make **adaptations** to their swimming strokes to compensate. Help your lifeguards learn to distinguish such swimming adaptations from signs of distress or drowning. Ask your lifeguard team to become familiar with patrons with disabilities who frequent your facility and the swimming strokes they use to better recognize any difficulty in the water.

In some cases, you or other lifeguards may help transport a patron with a motor impairment within the facility. You may also be responsible for the patron's entrance into and exit from the water. Make sure all lifeguards know where special equipment for these functions is located and how to use it (Fig. 7-10). You may teach this in in-service training.

Follow these guidelines when interacting with patrons with motor impairments:

- Look beyond the impairment and relate to each patron as an individual.
- Do not be afraid to tactfully ask a patron about his or her capabilities.
- When appropriate, wait until the patron asks for assistance. Respect the person's right to indicate what help he or she needs.
- Try not to categorize the patron by expecting only certain kinds of behavior or levels of achievement.

figure 7-10 *Staff need to know where special equipment is located and how to use it to help a patron with a motor function impairment.*

- Remember that people with disabling conditions are similar only in very general ways, and individuals will vary greatly in their conditions and capabilities.
- When assisting the patron in and out of the water, ask the patron how he or she would like you to assist. Let the person clarify where he or she needs support and what lift method is most comfortable.
- Be supportive but do not show pity.
- Be considerate. Speak directly to a person with a disability, not through a family member or peer.
- Allow patrons to keep **assistive devices** or **prosthetic devices** within reach. These devices may include a wheelchair, crutches, or an artificial limb.
- Do not ignore an obvious need, but do not overdo assistance.

As a head lifeguard, you may be responsible for helping lifeguards accommodate and communicate with patrons with various disabilities. Understanding the disabilities of patrons who frequent your facility will help you and your staff interact effectively with them.

SUMMARY

As a head lifeguard, your ability to interact effectively with the public depends on your training and experience as well as your facility's operating guidelines. By intervening in problem situations, respecting cultural differences, and appropriately accommodating patrons with disabilities, you help keep the environment safe and enjoyable for all patrons. You also help establish and maintain a well-trained lifeguard team. When you interact effectively with the public, you provide a powerful example for others to follow.

STUDY QUESTIONS

Circle the letter of the best answer or answers.
1. Which of the following guidelines contribute to a healthy relationship with patrons?
   a) Never insult or argue with patrons.
   b) Speak clearly and make direct eye contact.
   c) Only important complaints should be taken seriously and followed up.
   d) When talking to patrons, keep your sunglasses on.
   e) Be positive and nonjudgmental.
2. Which of the following is not an effective conflict management strategy?
   a) Arguing.
   b) Abandoning.
   c) Chance.
   d) Humor.
   e) Postponing.
   f) Sharing.
3. Which of the following basic guidelines should be followed when dealing with violent acts?
   a) As soon as you identify the violent act, call for assistance.
   b) Keep at least 2 feet of space between you and a violent person.
   c) Step between fighters with firmness; don't listen to arguments; stop the fight and arrange a cooling down period.
   d) Always intervene by yourself.
   e) Know who and how to grab to separate.
   f) If weapons are involved, do not approach the individuals involved. Call the police immediately.

4. Which of the following is not a good guideline for dealing with troublesome groups?
   a) Offer a friendly, accepting environment at your facility.
   b) Treat the group with respect.
   c) Treat each member as part of the group and not as an individual.
   d) Understand their language and idioms.
   e) Always give a group or an individual a way out with honor.
   f) Make them feel responsible.

Circle *True* or *False*.

5. If a patron causes problems as a result of bad behavior, you should eject the patron from the facility immediately. True or False?

6. When working with patrons who do not speak English, always try to communicate in English first. True or False?

7. When dealing with a hearing-impaired patron, you should shout to get his or her attention. True or False?

Fill in the blanks with the correct answer.

8. Patrons at your facility may have disabilities. Three categories of disabilities include _____ , _____ , and _____ .

9. Sequence the following steps for conflict resolution.
   ___ State what you want.
   ___ State the problem behavior.
   ___ Cool off.
   ___ Resolve the conflict.
   ___ State the feeling.

See answers to study questions on p. 121.

EMERGENCY RESPONSE

8

After reading this chapter, you should be able to—

1. Explain the responsibilities of the head lifeguard and support personnel during an emergency.
2. Explain why effective communication is needed during an emergency.
3. Describe four items to discuss when practicing an emergency action plan.
4. Explain the purpose and importance of an incident report.
5. List six categories of information that should be included on an incident report form.
6. Describe seven examples of procedures to follow after an emergency.
7. Explain what critical incident stress is and the effects it can have on a lifeguard or head lifeguard.
8. Recognize the signs of critical incident stress.
9. Describe six ways that a head lifeguard can cope with stress.
10. Explain the purpose of critical incident stress debriefing (CISD).
11. Define the key terms for this chapter.

Critical incident: Any situation that causes people to experience strong emotional reactions that can interfere with their ability to function.

Critical incident stress: The stress a person feels during or after a highly stressful emergency.

Critical incident stress debriefing (CISD): A process that brings the person or people who have suffered stress together with others who are trained to help them deal with its effects.

Emergencies: Sudden, unexpected incidents that demand immediate attention.

Incident report form: A report filed by a lifeguard or head lifeguard involved in any way in a rescue or other emergency.

Post-traumatic stress disorder: The condition in which a person is not able to cope, respond, or recover from the stress of a traumatic event.

INTRODUCTION

As a head lifeguard, you may develop different emergency action plans for the emergencies that might occur in your facility. Some plans may be similar; for example, evacuating the facility for a fire alarm may be the same as for a power failure. The facility may have one general plan to cover all related emergencies, such as all acts of violence, rather than separate plans for different acts of violence.

In all situations, the effectiveness of a plan depends largely on how well defined are the individual responsibilities of facility staff and management, communication channels, and follow-up procedures (Table 8-1). The most effective plans are frequently and thoroughly reviewed, practiced, and evaluated by both staff and management.

table 8-1 Contents of an Emergency Action Plan

Facility Layout	• EMS personnel access
	• Location of rescue and first aid equipment
	• Exits and evacuation routes
Equipment	• Rescue equipment
	• SCUBA
	• First aid supplies
	• Emergency equipment (flashlights, fire extinguisher, etc.)
Support Personnel	**Internal** / **External**
	• Cashiers / • Medical personnel
	• Clerical / • Police
	• Maintenance / • Fire
	• Hazmat (Hazardous materials) team
	• Poison control
	• Hospitals
	• Power company
	• Chemical supplier
	• Health department
Staff Responsibilities	• Each lifeguard assigned a duty
	• Rescue
	• Back-up coverage
	• Clear pool
	• Crowd control
	• Meet EMS personnel
Communication	• 9-1-1
	• Chain of command
	• Family/guardian
	• Media
Follow-up	• Replace equipment and supplies
	• Emergency action plan evaluation
	• Staff debriefing (procedural)
	• Critical Incident Stress Debriefing (CISD)—if necessary

TYPES OF EMERGENCIES

Different types of *emergencies* can occur at aquatic facilities (Table 8-2). Certain types of emergencies, such as specific natural disasters, are more likely in some locations than in others, but most emergencies can occur anywhere.

Aquatic emergencies include **distressed swimmers,** drowning, and spinal injuries caused by headfirst entries. Other emergencies include illnesses and injuries that occur in or out of the water. These include heart attack and other sudden illnesses, such as seizure and stroke, and injuries involving severe bleeding, fractures, and dislocations.

Certain emergencies result from a specific facility problem, such as a fire, power failure, disruption of telephone or other means of communication, or situations involving chemicals, such as a chemical spill.

Severe weather and **natural disasters** may involve violent winds, tornadoes, lightning, earthquakes, mud slides, and sudden floods.

A missing person is an emergency that can occur anywhere but is more likely at waterfronts where large groups of people may be spread over a wide area.

The facility's emergency action plans should address all these categories of emergencies. Each plan should define the responsibilities of everyone who may become involved.

table 8-2 Types of Emergencies

Water Emergency	• Distressed swimmer
	• Drowning
	• Spinal injury
Injury/Illness	• Sudden illness
	• Breathing emergencies
	• Wounds
Facility	• Fire
	• Power failure
	• Chemical spill
	• Telephone system failure
Natural Disaster/Weather	• Severe weather
	• Tornado
	• Thunder storm
	• Earthquake
People-Related Emergencies	• Missing person
	• Acts of violence
	• Riot

RESPONSIBILITIES

Everyone in the facility may have a role in an emergency, including all lifeguards and other staff. Support personnel outside the facility also have responsibilities in an emergency.

Lifeguarding responsibilities

As head lifeguard, you may be the one who decides which lifeguards or other staff have the following responsibilities:

• Who covers the rescuer's area
• Who clears the swimming area
• Who calls EMS personnel or other support if necessary
• Who meets EMS personnel, and where

You may also have to decide who has continuing responsibility after the emergency. An ***incident report form*** must be filled out as soon as possible. Someone must inspect and report the condition of any equipment and supplies used. Someone has to get written statements from witnesses. You have to designate who performs these and other tasks.

The head lifeguard's responsibilities vary depending on the type of emergency. With a missing person, for example, the head lifeguard often is the one who decides to search, identifies where to start the search, and oversees the water search operation, including public address system announcements.

In general, the head lifeguard must ensure the appropriate emergency action plan is functioning as intended. You need to be aware of what is happening at all steps in the plan and make sure the emergency is managed well. While lifeguards are following their prescribed steps, your job is to be on the spot, ready to fill in immediately if a problem develops or an unforeseen complication occurs. Your role should also be described in the emergency action plan.

Support personnel

Support personnel within the facility include all staff: cashiers, maintenance personnel, instructors, and others, though not all have a role in every emergency (Fig. 8-1). The emergency action plan describes everyone's responsibilities, and an additional **flow chart** of the chain of command should show lines of authority and responsi-

bility in the facility from top management on down. This includes everyone on staff, even part-time staff and coaches and instructors who use the facility periodically. The chart should show each person's immediate supervisor and the person to report to if that supervisor is absent.

Support outside the facility includes EMS personnel, fire fighters, law enforcement personnel, poison control centers, the power company, the chemical supply company, and other relevant external groups or agencies (Fig. 8-2). You may involve them when certain emergency plans are developed, and you may ask them to address lifeguards and other staff about their functions if

figure 8-1 *The responsibilities of support personnel in a facility during an emergency should be included in the emergency action plan.*

figure 8-2 *Include the responsibilities of support personnel from outside the facility in the emergency action plan.*

certain emergencies occur at the facility. You and your staff also need to know how long it normally takes these personnel to reach the facility in an emergency.

COMMUNICATION

Emergency action plans depend on good communication. In every plan, specify who communicates with whom (both inside and outside the facility), who is responsible for each communication, and when it takes place. The plan may even specify which telephone to use. For example, a plan designates who is to call EMS personnel, and directions are posted next to each telephone for how to talk to the dispatcher so that an excited or flustered caller can easily give the designated information. (See Appendix K for emergency telephone directions.)

The chain of command chart should also identify who in addition to EMS personnel needs to be notified in specified emergencies. It should also name the facility spokesperson who is to talk with the media, the public, and the family of a victim. Usually, someone experienced with the media has this important task. Staff must also know how to respond to the media, the public, and the victim's family in an emergency.

Communication within the facility is also important. Lifeguards and support staff should be very familiar with the signals lifeguards use to communicate with each other and other systems of internal communication. Have a backup system in case usual communications fail.

EMERGENCY PREPAREDNESS

To work effectively when an emergency does occur, emergency action plans must be practiced. When you talk with your lifeguards and other staff about your action plans for different types of emergencies, discuss the plans' advantages and any disadvantages. Encourage lifeguards to suggest any possible improvements in the plans. Be sure to discuss with the lifeguards the topics of reaction time, visibility, backup, and support personnel in and out of the facility. Lifeguards must know the difference between life-threatening and nonlife-threatening emergencies and know the procedures for dealing with both. Review first aid procedures and techniques regularly.

Practice your emergency action plans regularly during in-service training sessions. Periodically ask local emergency personnel to help you rehearse emergency plans, if possible (Fig. 8-3).

The facility

Post layouts of the facility where both lifeguards and the public can see them. This layout should show the location of the first aid area, rescue equipment, fire alarm

figure 8-4 *An example of a facility layout.*

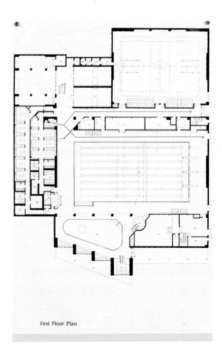

First Floor Plan

figure 8-3 *Practice your emergency action plans regularly.*

boxes, fire extinguishers, chemical storage areas, telephones, entrances and exits, locker rooms, showers, and storage. The layout should also show the evacuation route for the facility (Fig. 8-4).

Another layout, only for lifeguards, can show the lifeguard stations, surveillance zones, rescue equipment, and other items they should know in an emergency. A local map should also be available to lifeguards, showing police stations, fire houses, hospitals, rescue squads, and the power company.

Regularly check all facility telephones to make sure they are working. Be sure the emergency telephone numbers are posted by every telephone. Cover these lists of numbers with heavy clear plastic to protect them from weather and graffiti. If the facility does not have a separate first aid area, find an appropriate space and ask management to equip it with the necessary supplies. Make sure all facility staff know where this area is and where supplies are stored.

Equipment

The emergency action plan should also list all the rescue and first aid equipment in the facility and where it is located. Identify equipment for different types of emergencies. For example, a plan should specify the type of respiratory safety equipment the facility uses in a chemical spill. Recommend that management buy any additional equipment you believe is needed for safety purposes, and explain why it is needed. Make sure all equipment that may be used in an emergency can be easily reached and is in good working condition.

AFTER AN EMERGENCY

When the emergency is over and the victim has recovered or is being cared for by EMS personnel, you need to ensure follow-up procedures are completed. For example, you may—

- Continue to maintain crowd control if the water was cleared.
- Decide if the lifeguards can return to surveillance. If not, report to your supervisor. The facility may have to be closed.
- Inspect all equipment and supplies used in the emergency. Ensure all required equipment is in place and in good working condition before reopening the water area.
- Report the incident to management.
- If media reporters are at the facility, make sure that the designated spokesperson is handling the situation.
- Ensure witnesses have been interviewed before they leave the facility.
- Make sure necessary reports are completed and filed.

After an emergency, you, management, and other staff should evaluate how effective the emergency action plan was in this situation. Walk through the event with lifeguards and support personnel. Identify what worked well and what could have been done better. Then correct weak areas in the plan and build on the strengths. If the plan is changed, be sure to walk staff through the new version as soon as possible.

INCIDENT REPORTS

After an emergency, lifeguards involved must file an incident report. If there was a serious injury, witness statements are taken. These statements and reports document what occurred in the emergency. They are a record of what happened and can be used in court if there is later legal action. You and facility management can also review and analyze these permanent records to try to find ways to make the facility safer. Over time, these records may reveal hazards in the facility and what kinds of problems are most likely to occur. In addition, state or local governments or agencies usually require the facility to file incident reports.

Train your lifeguards to complete incident report forms correctly, accurately, and on time (Fig. 8-5). Many

figure 8-5 *An example of an incident report form.*

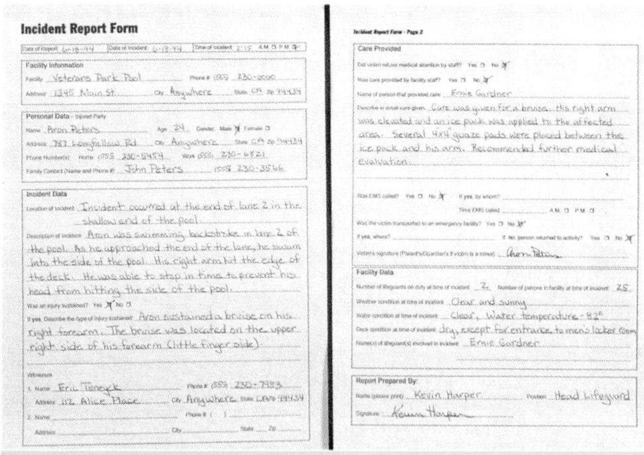

Incident Report Form

Facility Information
Facility: Veterans Park Pool
Address: 1345 Main St. City: Anywhere

Personal Data
Name: Aron Peters Age: 24
Address: 787 Longfellow Rd. City: Anywhere
Family Contact: John Peters

Incident Data
Location of incident: Incident occurred at the end of lane 2 in the shallow end of the pool.
Description of incident: Aron was swimming backstroke in lane 2 of the pool. As he approached the end of the lane, he swam into the side of the pool. His right arm hit the edge of the deck. He was able to stop in time to prevent his head from hitting the side of the pool.
If yes, Describe the type of injury sustained: Aron sustained a bruise on his right forearm. The bruise was located on the upper right side of his forearm (little finger side).

Witnesses
1. Name: Eric Teneyck City: Anywhere
Address: 112 Alice Place

Incident Report Form - Page 2

Care Provided
Name of person that provided care: Ernie Gardner
Describe in detail care given: Care was given for a bruise. His right arm was elevated and an ice pack was applied to the affected area. Several 4x4 gauze pads were placed between the ice pack and his arm. Recommended further medical evaluation.

Facility Data
Number of lifeguards on duty at time of incident: 2 Number of patrons in facility at time of incident: 25
Weather condition at time of incident: Clear and sunny
Water condition at time of incident: Clear, Water temperature - 82°
Deck condition at time of incident: dry, except for entrance to men's locker room
Name(s) of lifeguard(s) involved in incident: Ernie Gardner

Report Prepared By:
Name: Kevin Harper Position: Head Lifeguard

facilities use their own forms for recording incidents ranging from drowning to a problem with a disruptive patron. Some facilities have separate forms for incidents and injuries, and some also have a separate form for rescues. If your facility does not have any forms, you can develop one or more and make copies. Begin by looking over forms from other facilities, and then compose a form that works best for your facility. The sample incident report form shown in Appendix L can help you develop your facility's form.

Incident reports often classify injuries, assists, rescues, or submersion cases as major or minor. Incidents are classified further as water rescues, rescues requiring first aid, and rescues requiring CPR. State or local ordinances may require certain forms to be completed as soon as possible after an incident or injury.

figure 8-6 *Diagram for an incident report form.*

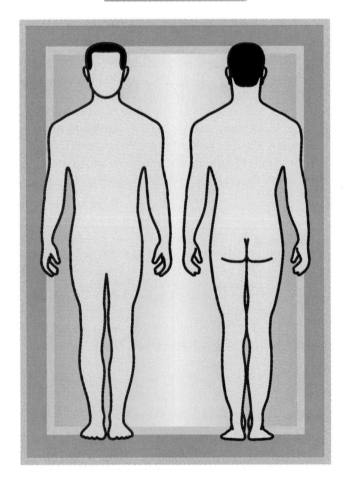

DIAGRAM FOR
INJURY REPORT

Many agencies and organizations use a checklist for identifying injuries. For example:

Location of injury:

☐ Head ☐ Trunk
☐ Neck ☐ Back
☐ Arm ☐ Leg
☐ Shoulder ☐ Foot

Another method uses front and rear diagrams of the body, on which the area of the injury is circled or checked (Fig. 8-6). These formats can be completed and read quickly. Some facilities use forms with a column for comments. Others ask the lifeguard to write a narrative description of what happened.

Help lifeguards understand they must be careful not to imply any fault for incidents, injuries, or fatalities in writing the incident report. Information must be as specific and factual as possible, without any suggestion of fault. Reports should contain only facts, not opinions. The lifeguard should not make any comments about how the incident could have been prevented or how staff could have acted differently.

Following are lists of information typically found on incident, injury, and rescue report forms. Some information is not needed at every facility. The facility's management may suggest what is priority information.

Information about the victim and the injury:

- The victim's name (With an unconscious victim, the person who identifies the victim should be identified by name, address, and telephone number.)
- The victim's address and telephone number
- Date of the victim's birth
- Sex of the victim
- Date and time of the report
- Date and time of the incident or injury
- Location of the incident: name and location of the facility
- Area of the facility in which the incident occurred: shallow water, deck, locker room, deep water, etc.
- Witnesses' names, addresses, and telephone numbers (Witnesses' statements should be on separate forms.)
- Type of injury: drowning, fracture, burn, etc.
- Location of injury: head, neck, arm, shoulder, etc.
- Type of activity: diving, running, swimming, etc.

- Description of the injury (including any equipment that may have been involved, such as a diving board or a deck chair)
- Condition of the victim (the final condition of the victim after the incident)
- First aid care given and by whom
- Taken from the facility by family or by whom (A signature is needed from whomever accepts responsibility for the victim, particularly with minors.)
- Whether victim left facility on his or her own (The signature of the victim or a guardian is required; with a minor, a witness should also sign the report.)
- Name and telephone number of family contact
- Whether transported to a hospital by EMS personnel

Information about the rescue, assistance, or care given:

- Type of rescue performed
- Distance to the victim: distance the lifeguard had to travel to get to the victim
- Number of lifeguards on duty
- Type of activity
- Assistance (any other staff who were involved)
- Equipment used: rescue tube, rescue board, backboard, etc.
- Care given? If not, why not? If so, what type? By whom?
- Rescue breathing given? For how long and by whom? If oxygen was given, by whom and for how long?
- Bleeding controlled? Care for shock? Bandage applied?
- CPR given? For how long and by whom?
- Spinal injury? (Describe complete care given, including the approach to the victim, how the victim was turned over in the water, and the application of a backboard.)
- EMS personnel called? By whom and at what time? Time of arrival? What did EMS personnel do? (Include names of EMS personnel and the location where victim was taken.)
- If the injury was minor (scrape, bruise) and the victim was released, a record of care given should be kept on file. This should include the victim's name, address, and telephone number. The victim, or relatives of the victim if the victim is a minor, should sign this record.

Information about conditions at time of injury:

- Weather: clear, cloudy, rain, temperature, electrical storm, fog, wind direction and wind velocity if possible, and so on.
- Water: temperature, clarity, and depth of water at the site of the incident (At a waterfront, include currents, whether the surface was calm or choppy, and beach conditions such as sandy, rocky, level, steep.)
- Number of people in the water and on the deck or beach at the time of the injury
- Lights: the total number of lights and the number on at the time of the incident (Include also for outdoors facility if overhead lights were in use.)

Information about decks or docks:

- Type: wood, concrete, tile
- Condition: wet, dry, broken
- Beach and grass areas: terrain surrounding the water, such as sunbathing areas

Information about the cause of the injury:

Have this information in the form of a checklist. Do not include space for opinions or judgments of the lifeguards or staff members as to the cause of the injury.

Information about the rescuers:

- Names, addresses, telephone numbers
- Location of the lifeguard at the time of the incident

Information on witnesses' statements:

- Names, addresses, telephone numbers of witnesses
- Date of statement
- Description of the incident (a narrative statement by witnesses about what they saw; witnesses should make statements in their own words without influence from staff)

As head lifeguard, you can periodically review and analyze your facility's reports of past incidents, injuries, and emergencies. These can help you understand possible hazards at the facility and what kind of problems are most likely to occur.

CRITICAL INCIDENT STRESS

An emergency involving a serious injury or death is a *critical incident*. The **acute stress** it causes for staff, especially the primary rescuer, can overcome a person's ability to cope. This is often called *critical incident stress*. You need to understand the powerful impact it can have. Acute stress usually results from dramatic or overwhelming experiences for lifeguards, such as an unsuccessful rescue or any similar event. If not managed, this acute stress may lead to a serious condition called *post-traumatic stress disorder*.

A person suffering from critical incident stress may become anxious and depressed, and be unable to sleep. He or she may have nightmares, nausea, restlessness, loss of appetite, and other problems. Some effects may appear right away, and others only after days, weeks, or even months have passed. People suffering from critical incident stress may not be able to do their job well. If a lifeguard does not recognize the problem or denies it, he or she may continue to guard but be unable to do so effectively. As head lifeguard, you may be the one who decides whether this lifeguard can return to duty or should receive help. You should also recognize your vulnerability and seek assistance when necessary.

Watch for the following signs of critical incident stress reactions (Fig. 8-7):

- Confusion
- Lowered attention span
- Poor concentration
- Denial
- Guilt
- Depression
- Anger
- Change in interactions with others
- Increased or decreased eating
- Uncharacteristic, excessive humor or silence
- Unusual behavior

If a lifeguard shows any of these signs, suggest that management arrange for professional help.

Look for these signs of critical incident stress.

figure 8-7

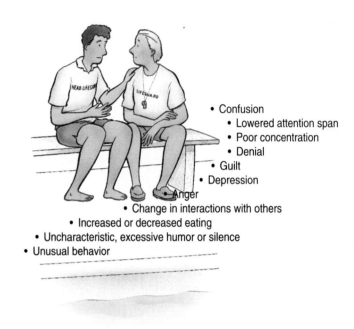

- Confusion
  - Lowered attention span
  - Poor concentration
  - Denial
- Guilt
- Depression
- Anger
- Change in interactions with others
- Increased or decreased eating
- Uncharacteristic, excessive humor or silence
- Unusual behavior

After a stressful incident, the person can do several things to reduce the effects of stress:

- Use quick relaxation techniques, such as deep, slow breathing.
- Eat a good meal.
- Avoid alcohol or drugs, including beverages with caffeine.
- Drink plenty of water.
- Review the event, and clear up any uncertainties.
- Attend a critical incident stress debriefing.
- Get enough rest.
- Get some type of physical exercise or activity.

An Emotional Rescue

When asked why you became a head lifeguard, you might first think of reasons like needing a summer job, making more money, being a leader, or wanting to help others. If you think more about this, you may realize you probably also have high expectations, are detail-oriented, need to control a situation, and are action-oriented and a risk taker. This is true of most men and women who become head lifeguards, just as for police officers who become sergeants, fire fighters who become lieutenants, or paramedics who become supervisors.

In part, people want to become leaders because of their high expectations and need for control. They like to direct and supervise others. With leadership, however, also comes more responsibility and stress. If a rescue does not succeed, someone gets injured, chemicals are spilled, your afternoon lifeguard does not show up, or one of your lifeguards has a problem, it is your problem.

Consider the following situation:

John is a head lifeguard in a facility having a very busy summer. Every day the pool is crowded, and the lifeguards are very active keeping everyone safe. Luckily, he has experienced lifeguards like Kevin. Last week, Kevin rescued a 6-year-old boy who followed his older brother into the deep end. When Kevin pulled the boy out, he wasn't breathing. Kevin thought he was dead and started rescue breathing. The paramedics arrived soon and were able to resuscitate the child. John is concerned because Kevin has been late to work every day since the incident and has been very quiet. The other lifeguards say he is not himself. He has not even talked about how well his baseball team is doing, which he used to talk about daily.

John is sitting in his office when the phone rings. It's Kevin, and he says he is not coming in to work that day. Kevin has never missed a day. John asks Kevin what is troubling him.

After a long silence, Kevin says, "I don't think I want to guard anymore. That kid last week, I should have spotted him sooner. He almost died, and it was my fault."

John, surprised by Kevin's comments, does not know what to say.

What has happened to Kevin? What can John do?

Kevin may be suffering from critical incident stress. If left unattended, the stress from a highly stressful situation builds up. It can eventually cause serious psychological and physical problems and disrupt the person's ability to carry out life's normal functions. Extensive studies have demonstrated the need of people in high-anxiety and stressful jobs to be able to share their feelings and better understand and cope with their emotions.

Pioneered by Jeffrey T. Mitchell, Ph.D., critical incident stress debriefings have been developed to help emergency personnel. They are conducted by special psychological support teams called critical incident stress debriefing (CISD) teams. Dr. Mitchell has trained and helped set up CISD teams throughout the United States and other countries since 1983. Today, there are more than 300 CISD teams worldwide. Their objectives are to help prepare emergency personnel to cope with job-related stress and the negative effects of overwhelmingly stressful events.

Today, services such as critical incident stress debriefings are increasingly accessible to non-traditional rescue personnel. Relief organizations like the American Red Cross now provide mental health services to their disaster relief workers. As a head lifeguard, you may want to talk with agencies in your area that have CISD teams. Seek their help in providing information to your staff about stress, and ask them to become part of your emergency action plan.

From Mitchell J, Bray G. *Emergency Services Stress*. Englewood Cliffs, NJ, 1990, Prentice Hall. For more information on CISD and Stress Management, contact: American Critical Incident Stress Foundation, P.O. Box 204, Ellicott City, Maryland 21043, (301) 750-0856.

figure 8-8 *A debriefing of lifeguards after an incident.*

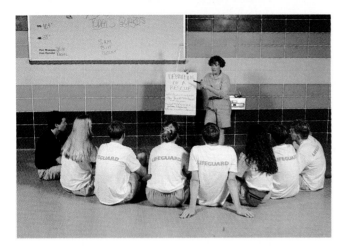

Hold a debriefing for everyone involved in the incident (Fig. 8-8). Talk about what happened. This may also help you identify individuals who may be having trouble coping with what happened. Let them know that events like rescues and caring for ill and injured people are overwhelming; that feeling upset is normal, natural, and not a sign of weakness; and that expressing their feelings is important. Listen carefully to see if a lifeguard is blaming himself or herself for what happened or for doing something wrong. That person may be experiencing critical incident stress. Remember that the effects of critical incident stress do not always appear right away. Watch for words and behavior that may indicate coping difficulties.

Ask your staff to watch for the signs of stress and to come to you if they experience them. Make sure they understand that coming forward does not reflect on their job performance or future ability to work. Sometimes staff hesitate to admit they are having trouble coping with an incident because of peer pressure, job performance expectations, or their self-image. Having a good rapport with your staff makes it easier for staff members to communicate with you. Lead by example, as well. Talk to your supervisor if you experience any difficulties in your position or in coping with an incident.

A process called ***critical incident stress debriefing (CISD)*** brings together people suffering critical incident stress with a trained **mental health professional** and **peers**. This process helps those suffering critical incident stress to share and understand their feelings and learn to cope. A CISD team usually includes peers such as other lifeguards or rescue personnel, who help create a less stressful atmosphere. These peers have received training for helping mental health professionals in conducting CISD.

After an incident involving severe injury or death, a CISD may be extremely important. Be sure you know how to contact mental health personnel when you need them. Emergency service agencies usually have CISD teams trained to respond and give critical incident stress debriefings. You or your facility management can arrange for them to help lifeguards when needed. Your facility's emergency action plans should include obtaining critical incident stress management for your staff.

SUMMARY

The head lifeguard has many responsibilities before, during, and after an emergency. To prepare for an emergency, the head lifeguard helps develop, practice, and evaluate the facility's emergency action plans and communication systems. If an emergency occurs, the head lifeguard makes sure that the facility's emergency action plan is effectively carried out. After the emergency, the head lifeguard makes sure everyone involved completes an incident report form and follow-up procedures. Because an emergency can be stressful, the head lifeguard should recognize the signs of critical incident stress so that he or she can arrange any necessary help.

STUDY QUESTIONS

Circle the letter of the best answer or answers.

1. The head lifeguard's primary responsibility during an emergency is to—
   a) Call and meet EMS personnel.
   b) Cover the rescuer's area.
   c) Clear the swimming area.
   d) Ensure that the emergency action plan for the specific emergency is functioning.

2. Unclear communication can cause an emergency action plan to fail. Which of the following steps can help improve communication?
   a) Identify who or what groups outside the facility must be called in specific emergencies.
   b) Identify who is responsible for each communication.
   c) Identify when communication should take place.
   d) Identify who should clear the swimming area.

3. Procedures that should take place after an incident include—
   a) Deciding if the lifeguards can return to surveillance duty.
   b) Reporting the incident to management.
   c) Ensuring that the designated spokesperson deals with the media.
   d) Identifying and interviewing witnesses before they leave the facility.
   e) Completing and filing all necessary reports.

4. When practicing an emergency action plan, items to discuss should include—
   a) The difference between life-threatening and nonlife-threatening emergencies.
   b) Worker's compensation.
   c) Reaction time.
   d) Support personnel.
   e) Visibility.
   f) Backup.

5. Incident reports can benefit a facility by—
   a) Showing who was at fault during the incident.
   b) Providing a record that can be reviewed and analyzed to make the facility safer.
   c) Recording what happened during the incident.
   d) Reducing insurance claims.

6. An incident report should not include information about—
   a) The victim and the injury.
   b) The rescue, assistance, or aid given.
   c) Conditions at the time of the injury.
   d) The cause of the injury.
   e) Who was at fault.
   f) Witnesses' statements.
   g) Opinion.

7. If critical incident stress is not taken care of, it can lead to—
   a) Pretraumatic stress disorder.
   b) Traumatic stress disorder.
   c) Post-traumatic stress disorder.
   d) Acute stress disorder.

8. The signs of critical incident stress include—
   a) Confusion.
   b) Lowered attention span.
   c) Poor concentration.
   d) Depression.
   e) Anger.
   f) Joy.
   g) Excessive humor or silence.

9. A CISD includes peers and a mental health professional to—
   a) Help those suffering from critical incident stress forget their problems.
   b) Help those suffering from severe depression to share, express, and understand their feelings.
   c) Help those suffering from critical incident stress to understand and cope with their feelings.
   d) Help those suffering severe anxiety to reduce their fear.

Circle *True* or *False*.

10. After a stressful incident, a cup of coffee followed by a beer will reduce the effects of stress and help you to relax. True or False?

See answers to study questions on p. 121.

LOOKING TO THE FUTURE

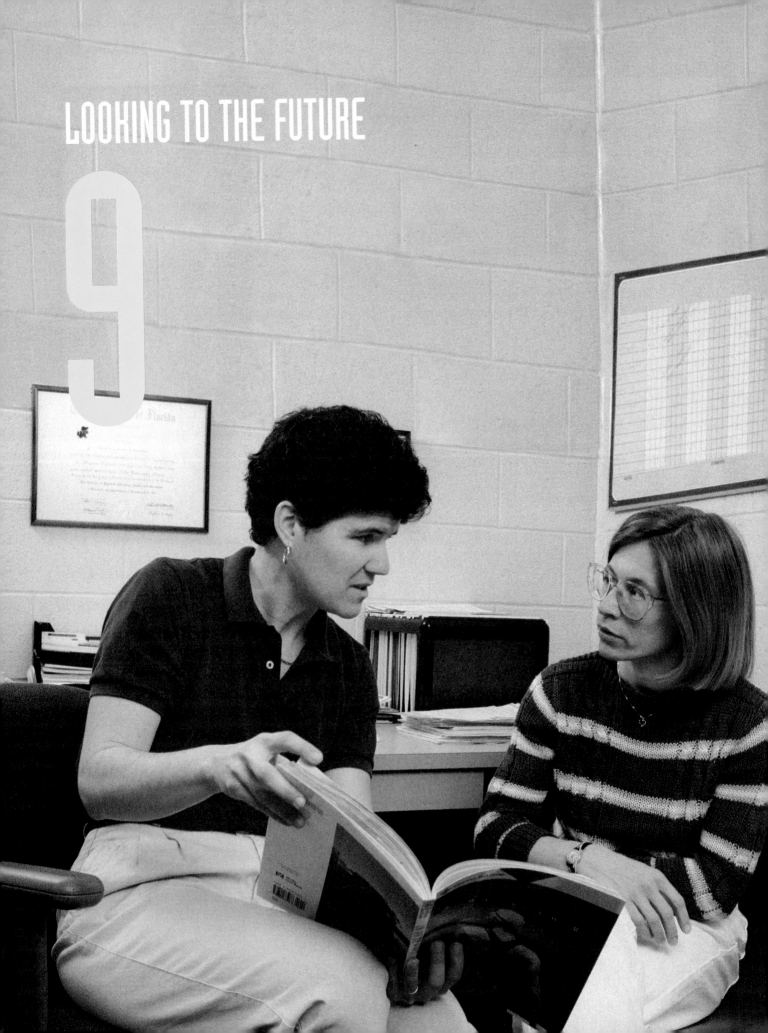

Objectives

After reading this chapter, you should be able to—

1 Explain how the experience and knowledge gained as a head lifeguard can be beneficial in future careers.

2 List at least five career opportunities in the aquatics field.

3 List four career opportunities in the recreation field.

4 List three college degrees to consider for a future career in aquatics.

5 Define the key terms for this chapter.

Key Terms

Aquatics consultant: A person with acquired expertise in the aquatics field who advises and solves problems in areas such as design, education, renovation, and risk management.

Career path: A direction taken within a chosen profession or occupation.

INTRODUCTION

I n this book, you have gained information about your roles and responsibilities as a head lifeguard. The head lifeguard position, however, may be only the first step of your journey on a *career path* in aquatics or recreation (Fig. 9-1). This knowledge will continue to be of value to you as you look to the future.

Your understanding of how risks are managed will become even more important if you move into higher positions, regardless of your specific career path in aquatics or recreation or the type of facility. Just as virtually all activities involve some risk that responsible managers seek to eliminate or minimize, most aquatic and recreational activities have potential for injury, and your risk management skills will be crucial.

Continue to build your knowledge and skills in selecting candidates for staff positions and training staff. In future positions, you may set employment criteria and make the hiring decisions, not only for lifeguards but for other staff as well. Your sensitivity to hiring issues will become more important as you assume greater responsibility for a facility or program and those who operate it. In future positions, you may supervise those who conduct in-service training. Your personal experience and training skills can be a support to your training staff and help them become knowledgeable and prepared for all aspects of their work.

The leadership skills you have learned and developed, both as leader of the lifeguard team and in your interactions with people, hold great value, not only for careers in aquatics or recreation, but for any career or life situation involving working with others. The ability to motivate others to do their best, for example, is just as important to an elementary school teacher or a bank president as to a head lifeguard. Whether or not you foresee a career possibility in aquatics or recreation, such as those described in the following sections, what you have gained will stay with you and contribute to your professional life and personal development.

figure 9-1 *Being a head lifeguard can be the first step of your journey on a career path in aquatics or recreation.*

CAREER OPPORTUNITIES IN AQUATICS

I f you are interested in continuing a career in aquatics, you will find the head lifeguard program has prepared you well. Employment as a head lifeguard can lead to many opportunities in the aquatics field. This experience has helped prepare you for a variety of positions in aquatic facilities (Fig. 9-2, A and B). Some of these positions include the following:

- **Pool Manager (Aquatic Facility Manager)**
  Oversees an aquatic facility's operation, which may include staffing, maintenance, and financial operation.
- **Aquatics Director/Superintendent/Supervisor**
  Oversees the operations of one or more aquatic facilities, which may include programming, maintenance, and financial operation.
- **Aquatics and Sports and Leisure Clubs Director**
  Oversees the operations of aquatics, sports activities, and leisure programs at a private health/fitness/racquet club or homeowners' recreation association.
- **Aquatics Programmer/Coordinator**
  Coordinates and plans a learn-to-swim program, water safety courses, lifeguarding courses, and special events.

- **Instructional Specialists/Swim Coach**
Includes instructors in specialty areas such as
SCUBA, springboard/platform diving, and water fitness, and coaches for competitive programs such as
springboard/platform diving, competitive swimming,
water polo, and synchronized swimming.

The experience you gain as a head lifeguard makes
the transition into management easier. You will also
have the inside track on hiring your facility lifeguards,
since you know how to identify the characteristics that
make a good lifeguard.

In addition to a specific position at an aquatic facility,
aquatics offers many other opportunities. What you
learn as a head lifeguard teaches you more than you may
realize about how a facility should be built and how it
should function. The aquatic consulting business is a
growing field. An *aquatics consultant* can provide an
aquatic facility with an objective review of operational
and safety procedures and practices; perform safety inspections and review maintenance practices; review the
facility's compliance with federal, state, and local regulations; and provide a review of staff performance. Both
public and private recreational businesses also need con-
sultants with aquatic experience to help design aquatic
facilities and programs and then advise them as to how
to administer them. Other opportunities include the following (Fig. 9-3):

- **American Red Cross Water Safety Specialist**
In larger American Red Cross units, positions are
often available for someone to coordinate learn-
to-swim, water safety, and lifeguarding courses
within the unit's jurisdiction. This person works
closely with local aquatic facilities and works directly with water safety instructors/instructor trainers
and lifeguarding instructors/instructor trainers and
provides them support.

- **Developer of Aquatic Materials**
You can help develop water safety and lifeguarding
programs and materials, such as books or videos,

figure 9-2 *A and B, Your experience can help prepare you for a variety of positions in aquatic facilities, such as a pool manager or a competitive swim coach.*

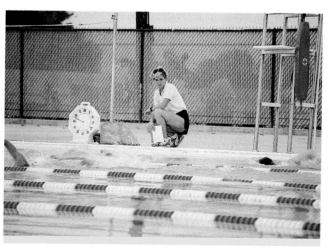

figure 9-3 *Other career opportunities in aquatics include developing aquatics materials and programs or lecturing on aquatics and safety.*

through local or national associations and private programs. If you gain enough experience in aquatics, you may eventually write aquatics material.

- **Aquatics and Safety Lecturer**
  This may include becoming an instructor at a college or university or giving presentations at aquatics conferences on your areas of aquatics expertise.

- **Graduate Assistant**
  Some colleges and universities offer graduate assistant programs in aquatics, recreation, physical education, and health. A graduate assistant is a college graduate student working on a masters or doctorate degree. The graduate assistant program allows the student to assist a professor by either helping with or teaching college courses. Colleges usually waive tuition fees and provide a stipend for the graduate assistant. Check with your college or university of choice for further information on graduate assistant programs.

CAREER OPPORTUNITIES IN RECREATION

Aquatics is only a small part of the overall recreation field. Full-time recreational personnel are needed at facilities at the national, state, and municipal level. Most **municipalities** in the United States also have recreation programs for children and adults (Fig. 9-4, A and B). Many private companies hire recreation specialists for their employee recreation and wellness programs. Your experience and knowledge as a head lifeguard can and will help you in any of these jobs. Some specific jobs in recreation follow:

- **Parks and Recreation Director**
  Oversees the total operation of the city or county parks and recreation department, which includes programming, maintenance of parks and facilities, and financial operation.
- **Recreation Program Supervisor**
  Oversees recreation programs, such as sports leagues, aquatics, self-development programs, and special events for a city or county parks and recreation department.
- **Recreation Center/Facility Manager**
  Oversees the operation of all facilities, including aquatics, sports, and parks, at a recreation center.

figure 9-4 *A* and *B*, *Programming and coordinating recreational activities is one aspect of a career in recreation.*

figure 9-5 *You may develop an interest in working as an emergency medical technician (EMT) or a paramedic.*

A

B

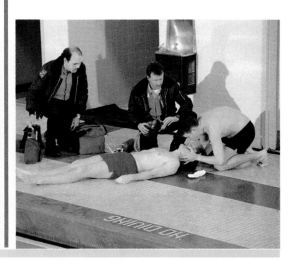

- **Recreation Specialist**
  Includes specialist positions in sports programming, therapeutic recreation, youth programming, senior citizen programming, and cultural arts. The person in any of these specialized areas coordinates or leads activities.

The recreation profession has adopted standards that make a college education a requirement for many positions. Although you may be able to obtain some positions in recreation without a college degree, the degree is almost always necessary for key positions. College degrees that you may consider when looking for a career in the recreation field include—

- **Recreation (Leisure Studies)**—private and commercial, general recreation administration, therapeutic recreation, sports management, and aquatics.
- **Physical Education (Human Performance)**— Exercise physiology, sport administration/management, secondary and elementary education, physical education–nonteaching track, and physical fitness management.
- **Health Education**—public, community health education, and health administration.

Check with colleges and universities to see what programs they offer. Professional organizations can also assist in providing you information on **accredited** programs and typical curriculum tracks at colleges and universities in a specific program area (see Appendix C).

Head lifeguard training is no substitute for a college degree, but some of the skills you have learned here will help you succeed in some of the courses you may take in college. In addition, much of what you have gained from this book can open the door to other career opportunities beyond those in recreation and aquatics.

OTHER CAREERS

From your experience as a head lifeguard, you may develop an interest in working as an **emergency medical technician (EMT)** or a **paramedic** (Fig. 9-5). Your first aid and CPR training and your education as a head lifeguard will help you prepare and adapt to a career in the emergency medicine field.

You can use the experience and education you gain as a head lifeguard in virtually any career you choose. Management and supervisory skills can be adopted and put to use in almost any occupation. Businesses are always looking for employees with experience in supervising and working with employees and the public. A head lifeguard position and the knowledge you gain from this book can give you a head start in the business world. There are no limits to what you can accomplish, even if you leave lifeguarding, aquatics, and recreation altogether. Set goals and do what it takes to achieve them.

STUDY QUESTIONS

Circle the letter of the best answer or answers.
1. Which of the following head lifeguard skills can be helpful to you in your future career choice?
   a) Risk management skills.
   b) Training skills.
   c) Leadership skills.
   d) Understanding of facility design and function.
2. Experience as a head lifeguard can lead to the following positions in aquatic facilities:
   a) Aquatics Director/Superintendent/Supervisor
   b) Aquatics Programmer/Coordinator
   c) Developer of Aquatic Materials
   d) Instructional Specialist/Swim Coach
3. Career opportunities in aquatics not attached to specific aquatic facilities include—
   a) Aquatics consultant.
   b) American Red Cross water safety specialist.
   c) Pool manager.
   d) Aquatics and safety lecturer.
4. Most careers in recreation require a college education. College degrees to consider for such a career include—
   a) Recreation (Leisure Studies).
   b) Applied Physics.
   c) Physical Education.
   d) Health Education.

See answers to study questions on p. 121.

ANSWERS TO STUDY QUESTIONS

Chapter 1

1. b
2. a, c, e
3. a, b, d
4. b

Chapter 2

1. d
2. a, b, c, d, f, g
3. a, c, e, f
4. b
5. a, b, c, d, e
6. b, c, d, e
7. a, b, d, e, f
8. a, b, c, d

Chapter 3

1. a, b, c
2. a, b, c, e
3. a, b, c, d, e
4. a, b, c, e, f
5. a, b, d, e
6. a, b, c, d, e, f
7. b, c, d, e
8. a, b, c, d, f, g
9. a, b, c, d, e, f
10. a, b, c, d
11. a, b, c, e
12. 1.b, 2.c, 3.a
13. 1.b, 2.b, 3.a, 4.a, 5.b, 6.a, 7.a, 8.a
14. False

Chapter 4

1. a, b, c
2. b
3. a
4. b
5. b
6. a, c
7. a, b, d, e
8. a, b, c

Chapter 5

1. b, c, d, f
2. b, c, d
3. a, b, c, d, e
4. a, c, e
5. a, b, d, f
6. a, b, c, e
7. b
8. c

Chapter 6

1. c
2. b; c; d
3. a; b; c
4. a; c; d; e
5. c
6. b; c; e; f
7. a; b; c; d;
8. 2, 6, 5, 1, 4, 3
9. False
10. False

Chapter 7

1. a, b, e
2. a, b
3. a, f
4. c
5. False
6. True
7. False
8. (In any order): Motor function, sensory function, mental function.
9. 4, 2, 1, 5, 3

Chapter 8

1. d
2. a, b, c
3. a, b, c, d, e
4. a, c, d, e, f
5. b, c
6. e, g
7. c
8. a, b, c, d, e, g
9. c
10. False

Chapter 9

1. a, b, c
2. a, b, d
3. a, b, d
4. a, c, d

HEAD LIFEGUARD TEXT
LIST OF APPENDIXES

SAMPLE DAILY LOG

Day: _____   **Date:** _____   **Hours of Operation:** _____

Opening Facility Inspection: _____

_____

_____

_____

Conducted By: _____   **Time:** _____

Closing Facility Inspection: _____

_____

_____

_____

Conducted By: _____   **Time:** _____

Staff Concerns: _____

_____

_____

_____

Patron Concerns: _____

_____

_____

_____

_____

Program Concerns: _____

_____

_____

_____

_____

Equipment Concerns: _____

_____

_____

_____

_____

Maintenance Concerns: _____

_____

_____

_____

_____

Other Concerns: _____

_____

_____

_____

_____

SAMPLE LIFEGUARD SCHEDULE

Week of _____ **to** _____
(M/D/Y)   (M/D/Y)

Lifeguard	Monday	Tuesday	Wednes-day	Thursday	Friday	Saturday	Sunday	Total Hours

SAMPLE LIFEGUARD SCHEDULE

Times	Monday	Tuesday	Wednesday	Thursday	Friday	Saturday	Sunday

ORGANIZATIONS AND ASSOCIATIONS
THAT PROMOTE AQUATICS

American Alliance for Health, Physical Education, Recreation and Dance (AAHPERD)
1900 Association Drive
Reston, Virginia 22091
(703) 476-3400

American Camping Association
Bradford Woods
5000 State Road 67 N
Martinsville, Indiana 46151-7902
(317) 342-8456

American Canoe Association
8580 Cinderbed Road, Suite 1900
P.O. Box 1190
Newington, Virginia 22122-1190
(703) 737-8300

American National Red Cross
Health and Safety Division
8111 Gatehouse Rd.
Falls Church, VA 22042
(703) 206-7180

American Swimming Coaches Association
301 SE 20th St.
Fort Lauderdale, Florida 33316
(305) 462-6267

Boy Scouts of America
1352 Walnut Hill Lane
Irving, Texas 75038-3096
(214) 580-2000

The Canadian Red Cross Society
1800 Alta Vista Drive
Ottawa, Ontario
Canada K1G 4J5
(613) 739-3000

The Commodore Longfellow Society
2531 Stonington Rd.
Altanta, Georgia 30338

Council for National Cooperation in Aquatics (CNCA)
P.O. Box 351743
Toledo, Ohio 43635
(419) 531-1025

Girl Scouts of America
420 Fifth Ave
New York, New York 10018
(212) 852-5720

International Swim and Dive Federation (FINA)
Avenue de Beaumont 9
Lausanne 1012
Switzerland

International Swimming Hall of Fame
1 Hall of Fame Drive
Fort Lauderdale, Florida 33316
(305) 462-6536

Jeff Ellis and Associates, Inc.
3506 Spruce Park Circle
Kingwood, Texas 77345
(713) 360-0606

National Collegiate Athletic Association (NCAA)
6201 College Boulevard
Overland Park, Kansas 66211-2422
(913) 339-1906

National Federation of State High School Associations
11724 Plaza Circle
P.O. Box 20626
Kansas City, Missouri 64195
(719) 464-5400

National Junior College Athletic Association
1825 Austin Bluffs Parkway
P.O. Box 7305
Colorado Springs, Colorado 80933-7305
(719) 590-9788

- **National Intramural and Recreational Sports Association (NIRSA)**
850 SW 15th Street
Corvallis, Oregon 97333
(503) 737-2088

- ★ **National Recreation and Park Association (NRPA) Aquatic Section**
650 West Higgins Road
Hoffman Estates, Illinois 60195
(708) 843-7529

National Safety Council
1121 Spring Lake Drive
Itasca, Illinois 60143
1-800-621-7619

National Spa and Pool Institute (NSPI)
2111 Eisenhower Avenue
Alexandria, Virginia 22314
(703) 838-0083

★ **National Swimming Pool Foundation**
10803 Gulfdale, Suite 300
San Antonio, Texas 78216
(210) 525-1227

The Royal Life Saving Society Australia
P.O. Box 1567
North Sidney, NSW 2059
02-957-4799
FX 02-929-5726

The Royal Life Saving Society Canada
287 McArthur Ave.
Ottawa, Ontario
Canada K1L 6P3
(613) 746-5694

The Royal Life Saving Society UK
Mountbatten House
Studley
Warwickshire
B80 7NN
0527 853943

Triathlon Federation/USA
3595 East Fountain Boulevard, Suite F-1
P.O. Box 15820
Colorado Springs, Colorado 80935-5820

United States Coast Guard (USCG)
Commandant (G-NAB)
2100 Second Street, S.W.
Washington, D.C. 20593-0001
(202) 267-1060

United States Coast Guard Auxiliary
3131 North Abingdon Street
Arlington, Virginia 22207
(703) 538-4466

United States Diving, Inc.
Pan American Plaza
201 South Capitol Avenue, Suite 430
Indianapolis, Indiana 46225
(317) 237-5252

United States Lifesaving Association (USLA)
425 East McFetridge Drive
Chicago, Illinois 60605
(312) 294-2332

United States Masters Swimming
2 Peter Avenue
Rutland, Massachusetts
(508) 886-6631

United States Power Squadron
P.O. Box 6568
Richmond, Virginia 23230
(804) 355-6588

United States Swimming, Inc.
1750 East Boulder Street
Colorado Springs, Colorado 80909
(719) 578-4578

United States Synchronized Swimming
Pan American Plaza
201 South Capitol Avenue, Suite 510
Indianapolis, Indiana 46225
(317) 237-5700

* **YMCA of the U.S.A.**
101 North Wacker Drive
Chicago, Illinois 60606
1-800-872-9622

YWCA of the U.S.A.
726 Broadway
New York, New York 10003
(212) 614-2700

World Water Park Association
P.O. Box 14826
Lenexa, Kansas 66285-4826
(913) 599-0300

• Professional Recreation Associations
* Organizations and Associations that offer pool operator programs.

SAMPLE FACILITY SAFETY CHECKLIST FORM

The Facility Safety Checklist Form provides a list of items in a facility that should be inspected on a regular basis. This form also provides a mechanism for follow-up action should something of concern be found

A sample of a facility safety checklist form follows that provides examples of some items that may be inspected at an aquatic facility. A blank form also follows and may be modified to fit your facility's specific needs. Other areas you may wish to include in your inspection are locker rooms and showers, pool furniture, diving boards and starting blocks, safety and first aid equipment, playground and picnic areas, and operational equipment.

After you determine the general areas you wish to include in your inspections, you must be very specific in listing what items to focus on when inspecting each general area. Chapter 3, "Aquatic Injury Prevention," can be used as a resource in developing your specific safety checklist forms. As an example, if you decide that locker rooms and showers are to be inspected, you would list specific items to focus on, such as—

- Standing pools of water and slippery surfaces.
- Leaky faucets, shower heads, and toilets.
- Broken locker room benches and chairs.
- Clogged drains.
- Water temperature too hot or too cold
- Broken floor or wall tiles.
- Damaged lockers.
- Damaged or non-functioning lights.
- Trash receptacles emptied and in place
- Fire extinguisher in place and functioning

Remember, proper documentation is vital to ensure a safe and healthy environment for your facility's patrons. These inspections can reduce obvious hazards and protect patrons from unnecessary injury.

SAMPLE FACILITY SAFETY CHECKLIST

	Yes	No	Action Taken	Date of Safety Check	Action Needed
1. Deck					
Safety equipment in good repair					
Rescue tubes and straps in good repair					
Backboards with head immobilizers and straps readily accessible					
First aid station clean; first aid equipment and supplies accessible and well stocked					
Telephones working properly					
Deck not slippery and in good repair					
Deck clear of patrons' belongings					
All equipment used by patrons stored properly if not in use					
Lifeguard stands clean and in good repair					
Clear of standing water					
Clear of glass objects					
2. Pool					
Ladders secured properly					
Ladder handles clean and rust free					
Steps not slippery and in good repair					
Ramp not slippery and in good repair					
Drain covers secured properly					
Drain covers clean					
Suction at drains not excessive					
Lifelines and buoys in order					
Water clarity satisfactory					
Water color satisfactory					
Pool free of debris					

SAMPLE FACILITY SAFETY CHECKLIST

	Yes	No	Action Taken	Date of Safety Check	Action Needed
1.					
2.					

SAMPLE PREEMPLOYMENT TEST FORM

Applicant's Name: _____

Facility's Name: _____

Date: _____ **Time:** _____

Test Administrator(s): _____ _____

Applicant's Certification (Attach copies of certifications with this form)

Lifeguarding	Date of Issue		*First Aid*	Date of Issue
☐ Lifeguard Training	_____		☐ Standard First Aid	_____
☐ Waterfront Lifeguarding	_____		☐ Community First Aid and Safety	_____
☐ Waterpark Lifeguarding	_____		☐ Responding to Emergencies	_____
CPR	_____		☐ Emergency Response	_____
☐ CPR for the Professional Rescuer	_____		☐ EMT	_____

Written Test Score (Attach copy of test answer sheet to this form)   _____

Applicants must have a score of 80% or better to be considered for employment.
If applicant did not pass the written test, he or she should not take the skills test.

Skills Test

The scoring system for the skills test is as follows:

Performance of Skill		Score
Unsatisfactory	=	1
Fair	=	2
Satisfactory	=	3
Good	=	4
Excellent	=	5

Score each skill based on this scoring system. Once the applicant has completed all the skills, total all scores to get the overall score. Applicant must score at least 80 points out of 100 possible in order to be considered for employment.

When scoring lifeguarding skills, score applicants on their entry, approach, skill performance, and removal from the water for each skill.

Sample Preemployment Test Form

First Aid Skills	Score
1. Controlling bleeding	____
2. Immobilizing a fracture of the arm	____
Subtotal score	____

CPR Skills	Score
3. Positioning a victim/Primary survey	____
4. Rescue breathing—adult	____
5. Rescue breathing—infant	____
6. Conscious choking adult	____
7. Unconscious choking adult	____
8. Unconscious choking infant	____
9. CPR—adult	____
10. CPR—infant	____
11. Two-rescuer CPR (beginning together)—adult	____
Subtotal score	____

Lifeguarding Skills	Score
12. Extension assist from the deck	____
13. Swimming extension rescue	____
14. Active victim rear rescue	____
15. Passive victim rear rescue	____
16. Submerged victim rescue	____
17. Head splint technique	____
18. Head and chin support technique—face down	____
19. Shallow-water backboarding	____
20. Deep-water backboarding	____
Subtotal score	____

First Aid Skills Subtotal	____
CPR Skills Subtotal	____
Lifeguarding Skills Subtotal	____
Overall Score	____

Applicant's Signature: _____ **Date:** _____

Test Administrator's Signature(s): _____ **Date:** _____

_____ **Date:** _____

LIFEGUARD RESCUE SKILLS

Condition	Rescue Skill
Distressed Swimmer	Extension assist from the deck
	Swimming extension rescue
	Active victim rear rescue
	Submerged victim rescue
	Rescue board rescue **(WF)**
	Simple assist **(W)**
Active Drowning Victim	Active victim rear rescue
	Submerged victim rescue
	Multiple-victim rescue
	Rescue board rescue **(WF)**
Passive Victim	Passive victim rear rescue
	Submerged victim rescue
	Rescue board rescue **(WF)**
Spinal Injury	Head splint technique
	Head and chin support—face up
	Head and chin support—face down
	Head and chin support—submerged victim
	Shallow water backboarding
	Deep water backboarding
	Spinal injury management in a winding river **(W)**
	Spinal injury management in a catch pool **(W)**
	Spinal injury management in a speed slide **(W)**

(W) = Waterpark skill   **(WF)** = Waterfront skill

FIRST AID AND CPR SKILLS

Condition	Rescue Skill
Bleeding	Controlling bleeding
Fractures	Applying an anatomic splint
	Applying a soft splint
	Applying a sling
	Applying a rigid splint
Appears Unconscious	Primary survey
Not Breathing	Rescue breathing
	Use of a resuscitation mask
	Use of a bag-valve mask (BVM)
Choking—Conscious	Abdominal thrusts (adult/child)
Choking—Unconscious	Abdominal thrusts (adult/child)
Not Breathing and No Pulse	CPR
	Two-Rescuer CPR, beginning together (adults and children only)
	Two-Rescuer CPR, changing positions (adults and children only)

GUIDELINES FOR ASKING NON-DISCRIMINATORY PREEMPLOYMENT QUESTIONS

Topic	What To Ask	What Not To Ask
Name	Have you ever gone by or used another name? Do we need more information about your name, change of name, or nickname to help us check references? If, yes, please explain.	Questions about maiden name. Avoid reference to marital status.
Residence	Where do you live?	Questions about owning or renting a home.
Age	Make a statement that you have to be ___ years old to work at facility. State that hiring is subject to verifying that applicant meets legal requirements. Are you over 18? If under 18, can you submit a work permit if hired? If hired, can you show proof of age?	Don't ask age or birth date. Don't ask for years of school (elementary or high) attendance. Don't ask questions that show applicant is over 40.
Birthplace, Citizenship, National Origin	Are you a U.S. citizen? What languages do you speak (if use of a different language is necessary- or important to the job)? If hired, can you verify your legal right to work in the U.S.?	Where were you born? What country are you a citizen of? What is your native language? Avoid all questions about ancestry, origin, descent, or parentage of applicant.
Race, Color		Questions about race, color, complextion. Color of eyes, hair, skin.
Disabilities	Make a statement that hiring may be contingent on passing a job-related physical examination. Do you have any impairments that would limit ability to do job? If so, are there accommodations that can address your limitation?	Questions about medical or health issues. Don't ask if applicant has a handicap or disability. Don't ask if applicant has received Worker's Compensation.
Arrest, Criminal	Have you ever been convicted of a job-related felony? Give details.	Questions about arrest record.
Military Service	Questions about job-related skills learned during military service.	General questions about military service or dates, type of discharge.
Travel, Child Care, Religion	Make statement about amount of travel or overtime or need for work consistency. State working days, hours or shifts. Can you work overtime? Is traveling a problem? If so, what is it?	Don't ask how family would feel about travel, hours. Don't ask about religion or family issues relating to schedule or travel. Avoid questions about pregnancy, child care, whether or not applicant has children or their ages. Avoid questions.

Topic	What To Ask	What Not To Ask
Organizations Activities, Clubs	Have job applicant give list of job-related clubs, organizations, societies, etc. Those indicating religious affiliation, color race, ancestry, age, or sex may be omitted.	Don't ask for comprehensive list of clubs, etc.
Sex, Marital Status, Economic Status		Don't ask if applicant is male or female, how he/she wants to be addressed (Mr. Ms. Mrs. Miss). Don't ask if single, divorced, separated or about spouse. Don't ask about assets, credit, bankruptcy, garnishment, or liabilities.
Physical Description	Make a statement that a photograph is required *after* employment.	Don't ask about height, weight. Don't require a photo before employment.

STATE HEALTH DEPARTMENTS AND REGIONAL OCCUPATIONAL SAFETY AND HEALTH ADMINISTRATION (OSHA) OFFICES

State of Alabama
Div. of Food & Lodging
434 Monroe
Montgomery, AL 36130-
3017
PH: (205) 613-5375

State of Alaska
Dept. of Environmental
Conservation (DEC)
Div. of Environmental Health
410 Willoughby Ave.,
Suite 105
Juneau, AK 99801-1795
PH: (907) 465-5280

State of Arkansas
Dept. of Health, State Bldg.
4815 W. Markham Street
Little Rock, AR 72205-3867
PH: (501) 661-2171

State of Arizona
Dept. of Health, State Bldg.
1740 W. Adams Street
Phoenix, AZ 85007
PH: (602) 542-1000

State of California
State Office Building 8
714 P Street, Room 600
Sacramento, CA 95814
PH: (916) 445-4171

State of Colorado
Div. of Engineering &
Sanitation
Department of Health
4210 E. 11th Avenue
Denver, CO 80220
PH: (303) 692-2000

District of Columbia
Dept. of Consumer &
Regulatory Affairs
614 H Street, NW Room 616
Washington, DC 20001
PH: (202) 727-7250

State of Connecticut
Frederick Adams Com.
Dept. of Health Services
150 Washington Street
Hartford, CT 06106-4474
PH: (203) 566-4800

State of Delaware
Division of Public Health
P.O. Box 637
Dover, DE 19903
PH: (302) 739-4731

State of Florida
Environmental Health
Programs
3401 West Thart
Tallahassee, FL 32303
PH: (904) 487-3166

State of Georgia
Dept. of Human Resources
522 Health Building
47 Trinity Avenue, SW
Atlanta, GA 30334
PH: (404) 657-9358

State of Hawaii
Dept. of Health
Sanitation Branch
591 Ala Moana Blvd.
Honolulu, HI 95813
PH: (808) 586-8000

State of Idaho
Environmental Health
707 North Armstrong Place
Boise, ID 83704
PH: (208) 327-7499

State of Illinois
Department of Public Health
535 W. Jefferson Street
Springfield, IL 62761
PH: (217) 782-4977

State of Indiana
State Board of Health
1330 W. Michigan Street
P.O. Box 1964
Indianapolis, IN 46206-1964
PH: (317) 633-0100

State of Iowa
Department of Public Health
Pool and Spa Program
Lucas State Office Bldg.
4th Floor
Des Moines, IA 50319-0075
PH: (515) 281-3032

State of Kansas
Dept. of Health &
Environment
Landon State Office Building
Topeka, KS 66612-1290
PH: (913) 296-1500

State of Kentucky
Dept. for Health Services
275 E. Main Street
Frankfort, KY 40621-0001
PH: (502) 564-4856

State of Louisiana
Dept. of Health & Human
Resources
325 Loyola Ave., Room 206
P.O. Box 60630
New Orleans, LA 70160
PH: (504) 568-5100

State of Massachusetts
Dept. of Public Health
Div. of Food & Drug
305 S. Street
Jamaica Plain, MA 02130
PH: (617) 727-2660

State of Maine
Div. of Health Eng.
157 Capitol Street
Station 10
Augusta, ME 04333
PH: (207) 289-5672

State of Maryland
Dept. of Health & Hygiene
3431 Benson Ave.
Baltimore, MD 21227
PH: (410) 646-9240

State of Michigan
Div. of Environmental
Health
3423 N. Logan Street
P.O. Box 30195
Lansing, MI 48906
PH: (517) 335-9216

Minnesota Health Dept.
Environmental Health Div.
925 Delaware Street, SE
Minneapolis, MN 55459
PH: (612) 627-5100

State of Mississippi
2423 N. State Street
P.O. Box 1700
Jackson, MS 39215-1700
PH: (601) 960-7400

Missouri Dept. of Health
Bureau of Community
Environmental Health
P.O. Box 570
Jefferson City, MO 65102
PH: (314) 751-6400

Department of Health &
Environmental Sciences
1400 Broadway
P.O. Box 200901
Helena, MT 59620-0901
PH: (406) 444-2408

State of Nebraska
Environmental Health
301 Centennial Mall, South
P.O. Box 95007
Lincoln, NE 68509
PH: (402) 471-2541

State of Nevada
Department of Human
Services
505 E. King Street
Carson City, NV 89710
PH: (702) 687-4750

State of New Hampshire
Dept. of Health & Human
Service
Occupational Health &
Safety
6 Hazen Drive
Concord, NH 03301
PH: (603) 271-2024

State of New Jersey
Consumer Health Services
3635 Quakerbridge Rd.
C.N. 369
Trenton, NJ 08625-0369
PH: (609) 588-3124

New Mexico Environment
Department
Liquid Waste Section
Ground Water Protection &
Remediation Bureau
1190 St. Francis Drive
P.O. Box 26110
Santa Fe, NM 87502
PH: (505) 827-2788

State of New York
Bureau of Community
Sanitation & Food
Protection
NY State Dept. of Health
1215 Western Ave.
Albany, NY 12203
PH: (518) 458-6706

State of North Carolina
Environmental Health
Services Section
P.O. Box 27687
Raleigh, NC 27611-7687
PH: (919) 733-9933

State of North Dakota
Department of Health
1200 Missouri Avenue
Bismarck, ND 58502-5520
PH: (701) 224-2370

State of Ohio
Local Environment Health
Services
35 E Chestnut
Columbus, OH 43266-0118
PH: (614) 466-1390

State of Oklahoma
Consumer Protection
Division
1000 NE 10th Street
Oklahoma City, OK 73117-
1299
PH: (405) 271-5245

State of Oregon
Environment Health
426 SW Stark, 2nd Floor
Portland, OR 97204
PH: (503) 248-3400

State of Pennsylvania
Dept. of Environmental
Resources
Bureau of Water Supply &
Community Health
P.O. Box 8467
Harrisburg, PA 17105-8467
PH: (717) 787-9035

State of Rhode Island
Department of Health
209 Cannon Building
3 Capitol Hill
Providence, RI 02908-5097
PH: (401) 277-6867

State of South Carolina
Bureau of Drinking Water
Protection
2600 Bull Street
Columbia, SC 29201
PH: (803) 734-4661

State of South Dakota
Dept. of Water & Natural
Resources
Office of Drinking Water
523 E. Capitol Street
Pierre, SD 57501-3181
PH: (605) 773-3754

State of Tennessee
Dept. of Health
Div. of Food & General
Sanitation
Tennessee Tower 12th Floor
312 8th Ave., North
Nashville, TN 37242-3901
PH: (615) 741-7206

State of Texas
Department of Health
1100 W. 49th Street
Austin, TX 78756
PH: (512) 458-7111

State of Utah
Bureau of Environment
Services
P.O. Box 16660
288 N. 1460 West
Salt Lake City, UT 84116-
0660
PH: (801) 538-6856

State of Vermont
Department of Health
60 Main Street
P.O. Box 70
Burlington, VT 05401
PH: (802) 863-7220

State of Virginia
Office of Environmental
Health
Main St. Station Suite 115
Box 2448
Richmond, VA 23218
PH: (804) 786-3559

State of Washington
CEHP
P.O. Box 47826
Olympia, WA 98504-7826
PH: (206) 586-8131

State of West Virginia
Environment Health Services
815 Quarrier St. Suite 418
Charleston, WV 25301
PH: (304) 558-2981

Wisconsin Division of Health
P.O. Box 309
Madison, WI 53701-0309
PH: (608) 266-8282

State of Wyoming
Environmental Health
Program
Hathaway Building, 4th Floor
Cheyenne, WY 82002
PH: (307) 777-7957

**OCCUPATIONAL
SAFETY AND HEALTH
ADMINISTRATION
REGIONAL OFFICE
ADDRESSES AND
TELEPHONE NUMBERS**

Region I
(CT, ME, MA, NH, RI, and
VT)
U.S. Dept. of Labor- OSHA
133 Portland Street, 1st Floor
Boston, Massachusetts 02114
PH: (617) 565-7164

Region II
(NJ, NY, and Puerto Rico)
U.S. Dept. of Labor - OSHA
201 Varick Street, Room 670
New York, NY 10014
PH: (212) 337-2325 or 2326

Region III
(DE, MD, PA, VA, WV and
the District of Columbia)
U.S. Dept. of Labor - OSHA
3535 Market Street
Gateway Building, Room
2100
Philadelphia, PA 19104
PH: (215) 596-1201

Region IV
(AL,FL, GA, KY, MS, NC,
SC, and TN)
U.S. Dept. of Labor - OSHA
1375 Peachtree Street, NE,
Room 587
Atlanta, GA 30367
PH: (404) 347-3573

Region V
(IN, IL, MI, MN, OH, and
WI)
U.S. Dept. of Labor - OSHA
230 S. Dearborn Street,
Room 3244
Chicago, Illinois 60604
PH: (312) 353-2220

Region VI
(AR, LA, NM, OK, and TX)
U.S. Dept. of Labor - OSHA
525 Griffin Street, Room 602
Dallas, Texas 75202
PH: (214) 767-4731

Region VII
(IA, KS, MO, and NE)
U.S. Dept. of Labor - OSHA
911 Walnut Street, Room 406
Kansas City, MO 64106
PH: (816) 426-5861

Region VIII
(CO, MT, ND, SD, UT, and
WY)
U.S. Dept. of Labor - OSHA
1961 Stout Street,
Room 1576
Denver, CO 80294
PH: (303) 844-3061

Region IX
(AZ, CA, HI, NV, American
Samoa, Guam, and the
Pacific Islands)
U.S. Dept. of Labor - OSHA
71 Stevenson Street,
Suite 420
San Francisco, CA 94105
PH: (9415) 744-7107

Region X
(AK, ID, OR, and WA)
U.S. Dept. of Labor - OSHA
1111 Third Avenue,
Suite 715
Seattle, WA 98101-3212
PH: (206) 553-5930

SAMPLE IN-SERVICE TRAINING REPORT

Facility Name: _____

In-service Location: _____

Date: _____ Time: (From/To) _____

In-service Instructor(s): _____

American Red Cross Instructor's Certification: ☐ LGI ☐ WSI ☐ CPRI ☐ FAI
☐ Other (list) _____

In-Service Topics

☐ CPR/FA (List Skills) _____

☐ Spinal Injury Management (List Skills) _____

☐ Rescues (List Skills) _____

☐ Conditioning (List) _____

☐ Other (Explain) _____

Participating Staff (Please Print):   ## Signature

1.) _____   _____

2.) _____   _____

3.) _____   _____

4.) _____   _____

5.) _____   _____

6.) _____   _____

7.) _____   _____

8.) _____   _____

9.) _____   _____

10.) _____   _____

SAMPLE LIFEGUARD EVALUATION FORM

Name of Lifeguard: _____

Facility: _____

Period covered by this evaluation: _____ to _____

The evaluation process should result in clear understandings of strengths and weaknesses and should lead to the establishment of a program so that weak areas can be improved and strengths built upon.

Performance Indicators: 1 = Unsatisfactory　2 = Marginal　3 = Satisfactory
4 = Good　5 = Excellent

Performance Factors	Qualifications	1	2	3	4	5
Job Knowledge	Has an understanding of all phases of his/her work.					
Lifeguarding Skills	Demonstrates competency in lifeguarding skills and techniques.					
Development	Participation in in-service trainings and staff meetings.					
Cooperation and Attitude	Ability to work with others and carry out instructions.					
Attendance	Consistency in avoiding absenteeism and tardiness. Secures a substitute if absent.					
Dependability	Works conscientiously according to instructions.					
Judgment	Ability to handle emergency situation when they arise.					
Patron Relations	Is courteous, professional, alert, and tactful.					
Rules Enforcement	Applies rules and regulations with consistency.					
Initiative	Ability to act on his/her own and take the lead.					
Appearance	Is clean and wears appropriate uniform.					
Overall Work Performance	Evaluation of individual's performance during this evaluation period.					

Supervisor comments:

Lifeguard comments:

Supervisor Signature: _____ Date: _____

Lifeguard Signature: _____ Date: _____

Signature of lifeguard indicates that this evaluation was seen and reviewed by the lifeguard but does not imply agreement.

INSTRUCTIONS FOR EMERGENCY TELEPHONE CALLS

Emergency Telephone Numbers [Dial __ for outside line]

EMS _____ Fire _____ Police _____

Poison Control Center _____ Number of this telephone _____

Other Important Telephone Numbers

Facility manager _____ Telephone number _____

Facility maintenance _____ Telephone number _____

Chemical company _____ Telephone number _____

Power company _____ Telephone number _____

Weather bureau _____ Telephone number _____

Name and address of medical facility with 24-hour emergency cardiac care: _____

_____

Information for Emergency Call
(Be prepared to give this information to the EMS dispatcher.)

1. Location _____

   Street Address _____

   City or Town _____

   Directions (cross streets, roads, landmarks, etc.) _____

_____

2. Telephone number from which the call is being made

3. Caller's name

4. What happened?

5. How many people injured?

6. Condition of victim(s)

7. Help (first aid) being given

Note: Do not hang-up first. Let the EMS dispatcher hang up first.

SAMPLE INCIDENT REPORT FORM

Date of report: _____ Date of Incident: _____ Time of Incident: _____ A.M. ☐ P.M. ☐

Facility Information

Facility: _____ Phone #: (   ) _____

Address: _____ City _____ State _____ Zip _____

Personal Data–Injured Party

Name: _____ Age: _____ Gender: Male ☐ Female ☐

Address: _____ City _____ State _____ Zip _____

Phone Number(s): Home (   ) _____ Work (   ) _____

Family Contact (Name and Phone #): _____ (   ) _____

Incident Data

Location of Incident: _____

_____

Description of Incident: _____

_____

_____

_____

Was an injury sustained? Yes ☐   No ☐

If **yes,** describe the type of injury sustained: _____

_____

_____

Witnesses

1. Name: _____ Phone #: (   ) _____

    Address: _____ City _____ State _____ Zip _____

2. Name: _____ Phone #: (   ) _____

    Address: _____ City _____ State _____ Zip _____

Care Provided

Did victim refuse medical attention by staff?   Yes ☐   No ☐

Was care provided by facility staff?   Yes ☐   No ☐

Name of the person that provided care: _____

Describe in detail care given: _____

_____

_____

_____

_____

Was EMS called?   Yes ☐   No ☐   If **yes,** by whom? _____

Time EMS called: _____   A.M. ☐   P.M. ☐

Was the victim transported to an emergency facility?   Yes ☐   No ☐

If **yes,** where? _____   If **no,** person returned to activity?   Yes ☐   No ☐

Victim's signature (Parent's/Guardian's if victim is a minor): _____

Facility Data

Number of lifeguards on duty at time of incident: _____   Number of patrons in facility at time of incident: _____

Weather condition at time of incident: _____

Water condition at time of incident: _____

Deck condition at time of incident: _____

Name(s) of lifeguard(s) involved in incident: _____

_____

Report Prepared By:

Name (please print): _____   Position: _____

Signature: _____

GLOSSARY

A

Abandonment Ending care of an ill or injured person without that person's consent or without ensuring that someone with equal or greater training will continue that care.

Abrasion An open wound in which skin is rubbed or scraped away.

Accommodations Arrangements to help people with disabilities participate in programs and activities.

Accredited Having official authorization or approval.

Acute stress Extremely severe stress.

Adaptations Things or actions that change are changed for a new or special use or situation, such as a swimming stroke of a person with a disability.

Aerobic exercise Sustained, rhythmic, physical exercise that requires additional effort by the heart and lungs to meet the increased demand by the skeletal muscles for oxygen.

Aerobic (oxygen-using) energy system The energy system in the body that breaks down carbohydrates, fats, and proteins for energy.

Anaerobic exercise Exercise at an intensity such that oxygen is not supplied consistently. Anaerobic exercise involves high intensity activity that lasts 2 minutes or less.

Anaerobic (without oxygen) energy system The energy system in the body that uses the most rapidly available source of energy—sugars and carbohydrates stored in the body—for muscular activity.

Aquatics consultant A person with acquired expertise in the aquatics field who advises and solves problems in areas such as design, education, renovation, and risk management.

Area of responsibility The zone or area for which a lifeguard conducts surveillance.

Assets The structures, property, other physical components, or anything of cash value of a business, person, corporation, or facility, plus any revenue generated.

Assistive devices Devices, such as wheelchairs, that help people with certain disabilities to function.

B

Backup coverage The expansion of other lifeguards' areas of responsibility when one lifeguard is taken away from his or her surveillance to perform a rescue.

Behavioral interviewing techniques Asking an applicant to describe a real event in his or her life.

Blind spot An area that cannot be seen or is difficult to see from a lifeguard station.

Breach of duty The infraction or violation of a law, obligation, or standard.

Bulkhead A movable wall placed in a swimming pool to separate activities or water of different depths.

C

Cardiovascular Pertaining to or involving the heart and blood vessels.

Career path A direction taken within a chosen profession or occupation.

Catch pool A small pool at the bottom of a slide where patrons enter water deep enough to cushion their landing.

Cerebral palsy A central nervous system dysfunction in which a person has little or no control of the muscles.

Certification A process in which a person demonstrates specific knowledge, competency, and skills and receives a certificate to that effect.

Chain of command The structure of employee and management positions in a facility.

Communication A process of passing information or ideas from one individual to another.

Competencies Capabilities.

Concussion A temporary impairment of brain function, usually without permanent damage to the brain; often caused by a blow to the head.

Confidentiality Protecting a victim's privacy by not revealing any personal information you learn about the victim except to law enforcement personnel or EMS personnel caring for the victim.

Consent Permission to provide care given by an ill or injured person to a rescuer.

Contractual Relating to a binding agreement between two or more people.

Cornerstone A main or essential basis.

Criteria Standards on which a judgments can be based.

Critical incident Any situation that causes people to experience unusually strong emotional reactions that interfere with their ability to function.

Critical incident stress The stress a person experiences during or after a highly stressful emergency.

Critical incident stress debriefing (CISD) A process that brings the person or people who have suffered stress together with others who are trained to help them deal with its effects.

Cultural diversity Differences among groups of people related to cultural background and exemplified through customs, beliefs, and practices.

D

Defuse To make less tense or harmful.

Delegation The process of entrusting others with tasks for which you are responsible.

Disability The loss, absence, or impairment of sensory, motor, or mental function.

Distressed swimmer A person capable of staying afloat but likely to need assistance to get to safety.

Duty to act A legal responsibility of certain people to provide a reasonable standard of emergency care; may be required by case law, statute, or job description.

E

Emergencies Sudden, unexpected incidents demanding immediate attention.

Emergency action plan A written plan detailing how facility staff are to respond in a specific type of emergency.

Emergency medical technician (EMT) A person who has successfully completed a state-approved Emergency Medical Technician training program; paramedics are the highest level of EMTs.

Escalate Increase, enlarge, intensify.

F

Facility manager The person who oversees an aquatic facility's operation, which may include staffing, maintenance, and financial operation.

Flow chart A structural diagram of a sequence of positions and/or operations, such as a chain of command.

Freestyle A competitive event in which any stroke is allowed. The term is frequently used for the front crawl, since that is the stroke most often used in this event.

G

Good Samaritan laws Laws that protect people who willingly give emergency care without accepting anything in return.

Ground fault interrupter (GFI) A device designed to eliminate the danger of electric shock or electrocution.

H

Head lifeguard A lifeguard who has a supervisory position in a facility's chain of command.

Hearing impairment Partial or total loss of hearing.

I

Implied consent A legal concept assuming that persons who are unconscious or so severely injured that they cannot respond would consent to receive emergency care.

In-service training Regularly scheduled staff meetings and practice sessions that cover lifeguarding information and skills.

Incentive Something, such as an expectation of an award, that motivates a person to act.

Incident report form A report filed by a lifeguard or head lifeguard involved in any way in a rescue or other emergency.

Industry standards The models set up by a business or organization, or an authority as rules by which to measure something, such as quality of care.

Informed consent Permission the victim, parent, or guardian gives the rescuer to provide care. This consent requires the rescuer to explain his or her level of training, what the rescuer thinks is wrong, and the care the rescuer intends to give.

Infraction When a rule is intentionally or unintentionally broken.

Insurance underwriter A person who assumes the risk of paying for a loss or damage for which someone or group is insured.

Interpersonal Among or between people.

L

Laceration A cut, usually from a sharp object; may have jagged or smooth edges.

Lawsuit A legal procedure for settling a dispute.

Leadership style The manner in which one person interacts with and leads other people.

Liability insurance Insurance that protects against the bad consequences of the action of any representative of a business, agency, organization, or corporation.

Liaison Communication between groups or units; one who establishes or maintains a close bond or connection.

Lifeguard evaluation form A form used to evaluate and document a lifeguard's performance level.

Lifeguard team Two or more lifeguards, including the head lifeguard as team leader, who work and interact together as a group.

Literacy The ability to read and write.

M

Mainstreaming Including people with disabilities in the same programs and activities as the non-disabled.

Material Safety Data Sheet (MSDS) A form that provides information about a hazardous substance.

Mental function The brain's capacity to acquire and apply information.

Mental health professional People whose jobs focus on improving the mental and emotional well being of others.

Molestation An interference or persecution with hostile intent.

Motor function The brain's ability to direct purposeful physical activities.

Multiple sclerosis A progressive disease characterized by patches of hardened tissue in the brain or spinal cord.

Municipalities A political unit, usually urban and usually having powers of self government.

Muscular dystrophy A hereditary disease characterized by progressive deterioration of muscles, leading to disability, deformity, and loss of strength.

N

Natural disasters   The catastrophic results of forces or events caused by nature, such as earthquakes, floods, and tornadoes.

Negligence   The failure to provide the level of care a person of similar training would provide, thereby causing injury or damage to another.

O

Occupational Safety and Health Administration (OSHA)   A government agency that helps protect the health and safety of employees in the workplace.

Ordinances   Local government regulations.

Orientation   A meeting to familiarize new employees with all aspects of the workplace and their job responsibilities.

P

Pantomiming   Conveying a message by body movements only.

Paralysis   A loss of muscle control; a permanent loss of feeling and movement.

Paramedic   A highly specialized EMT.

Patron loads   The maximum number of patrons that health codes permit to be in a facility or a pool at one time.

Peers   People who have equal standing with each other.

Performance evaluation   A process that determines how well an individual is performing in his or her job duties.

Performance level   The ability to execute skills and demonstrate knowledge relative to the standards and expectations of the job.

Physiology   A branch of biology that deals with the functions and activities of life and living matter.

Post-traumatic stress disorder   A condition in which a person is not able to cope, respond, or recover from the stress of an emotionally shocking event.

Preemployment process   The series of actions that take place before an applicant is hired.

Preemployment test form   A form that documents an applicant's certification and test results before he or she becomes employed.

Problem-solving skills   The ability to develop effective solutions for difficult situations

Prosthetic devices   Artificial devices to replace missing body parts.

R

Refusal of care   The declining of care by a victim; the victim has the right to refuse the care of anyone who responds to an emergency.

Risk management   Identifying, eliminating, or minimizing dangerous conditions that can cause injuries and financial loss.

Rotation   The scheduled moving of lifeguards for surveillance purposes from one lifeguard stand or other area to another.

S

Safety team   A network of people in the facility and EMS system who can respond to and assist a lifeguard in an emergency.

Scanning   A visual technique used by lifeguards to properly observe and monitor patrons participating in water activities.

Self-contained breathing apparatus   A unit with an air supply tank, mask, and controls used by a person entering an area where the air is unsafe to breathe.

Sensors   A device that receives and responds to a signal or stimulus.

Sensory function   The ability to hear, see, touch, taste, and smell.

Simulation   A lifelike teaching situation in which individuals or a whole team work to solve a given problem.

S.M.A.R.T. goal   A goal that in **S**pecific, **M**easurable, **A**ttainable, **R**elevant, and **T**ime oriented.

Software   Computer programs.

Spa   A small pool or tub in which people sit in rapidly circulating hot water.

Sprints   Short distances in which a swimmer swims at top speed.

Standard of care   The minimal standard and quality of care expected of an emergency care provider.

Strategies   A plan of action.

Surveillance   A close watch kept over someone or something, such as patrons and the facility.

Synchronized swimming   Rhythmical water activity of one or more people performed in a pattern synchronized to music.

T

Tactile impairment   Partial or total loss of the sense of touch.

Teamwork   An attitude and a shard sense of spirit in a group of individuals.

Therapeutic   Pertaining to the treatment of disease or the art of healing.

Therapy pool   A pool in a facility specifically used for medically-prescribed treatment and rehabilitation.

V

Vantage point   A position or standpoint from which something is viewed or considered.

Velocity   The rate or speed of an action or motion.

Vision impairment   Partial or total loss of sight.

W

Workers compensation   An amount of money paid by a group, business, or organization to an employee who is injured on the job.

Z

Zones   A section or division of an area established for a specific purpose. *See also* Area of Responsibility.

REFERENCES

The American National Red Cross *Adapted Aquatics, Swimming for Persons with Physical or Mental Impairments*. The American National Red Cross, Washington, D.C., 1977.

_____. *Emergency Response*. Mosby, St. Louis, Missouri, 1993.

_____. *Lifeguarding*. American Red Cross, Washington, D.C., 1990.

_____. *Lifeguarding Today*. Mosby, St. Louis, Missouri, 1994.

_____. *Personnel Practices for Supervisors*.

_____. *Swimming and Diving*. Mosby, St. Louis, Missouri, 1992.

_____. *Water Safety Instructor's Manual*. Mosby, St. Louis, Missouri, 1992.

C.L. Smith Elementary School. *Problem Solving*. San Luis Coastal Union School District, San Luis Obispo, California, 1993.

Department of Recreation and Conservation. *Swimming Pool Management Manual*. Commonwealth of Pennsylvania, Harrisburg, Pennsylvania, 1993.

Ebben, A. *Pool Lifeguarding*. Studley, Warwickshire, England: The Royal Life Saving Society, United Kingdom, 1993.

Ellis, Jeff and Associates, Ellis and Associates/*National Pool and Water Park Lifeguard Training* manual, 1993.

Gabrielsen, M.A. *Swimming Pools: A Guide to Their Planning, Design, and Operation*. Human Kinetics Publishers, Champaign, Illinois, 1987.

Hafen, B., and Karren, K. *Prehospital Emergency Care and Crisis Intervention*. Motron Publishing Company, Englewood, Colorado, 1989.

Johnson, R.L. *YMCA Pool Operations Manual*. Human Kinetics Publishers, Champaign, Illinois, 1989.

Kowalsky, L., editor *Pool-Spa Operators Handbook*. San Antonio, Texas: National Swimming Pool Foundation, 1990.

Mull, F., Bayless, K. and Ross, C. *Recreational Sports Programming: Sports for All*. The Athletic Institute, North Palm Beach, Florida, 1987.

Staley, E., Meyers, R., and Gomez, A. *Guiding the Development of Youth Behavior in Recreational Settings*. Recreation and Youth Services Planning Council, Los Angeles, California, 1972.

Washington State Public Health Association. *Manual: Swimming Pool Operation*. Washington State Public Health Association, Seattle, Washington, 1985.

YMCA of the USA. *Aquatics For Special Populations*, Human Kinetics, Champaign, Illinois, 1987.

YMCA of the USA. *On the Guard YMCA Lifeguard Manual*. Human Kinetics, Champaign, Illinois, 1986.

INDEX

American Red Cross
Head Lifeguard Course

Instructor(s)_____

_____

Please take a few moments to tell us how well we met your expectations.

Mark one oval on each line to show how much you agree or disagree with the following:

Agree ▶ ▶ ▶ ▶ ▶ Disagree

#	Question	1	2	3	4	5
1	Instructor was well prepared and professional.	①	②	③	④	⑤
2	Instructor was clear and understandable.	①	②	③	④	⑤
3	Book was clear and easy to follow.	①	②	③	④	⑤
4	The study questions in the book were helpful.	①	②	③	④	⑤
5	The classroom was clean and orderly.	①	②	③	④	⑤
6	The activities I participated in were appropriate.	①	②	③	④	⑤
7	Time for activities was adequate.	①	②	③	④	⑤
8	Instructor was helpful during activities sessions.	①	②	③	④	⑤
9	Location was convenient.	①	②	③	④	⑤
10	Course was a good value for the price.	①	②	③	④	⑤
11	I would recommend this course to a friend.	①	②	③	④	⑤

12 How satisfied are you that you learned enough to put this information into practice?

○ Very satisfied ○ Dissatisfied
○ Satisfied ○ Very dissatisfied
○ Neither satisfied nor dissatisfied

13 Overall, how satisfied are you with the training provided?

○ Very satisfied
○ Satisfied
○ Neither satisfied nor dissatisfied
○ Dissatisfied
○ Very dissatisfied

14 Did you register for this course yourself?
○ Yes ▶ ▶ Go to Question 15.
○ No ▶ ▶ Skip to Question 17.

Agree ▶ ▶ Disagree

15 Registration process was efficient and easy. ① ② ③ ④ ⑤

Agree ▶ ▶ Disagree

16 Red Cross staff was polite and helpful. ① ② ③ ④ ⑤

17 How did you find out about this course? *(Mark all that apply.)*

○ Employer   ○ Friend or neighbor
○ Poster   ○ Local Red Cross unit
○ Newspaper   ○ Other ▶ How?
○ Radio or TV   _____

18 Why did you decide to take this course? *(Mark one.)*

○ Job requirement
○ Another reason   Why? _____

19 If you took this course for a job requirement, where do you expect to work as a head lifeguard? *(Mark one.)*
○ Pool   ○ Waterpark
○ Beach (Ocean)   ○ Don't know/Not sure
○ Waterfront (Lake)

20 Have you ever worked as a lifeguard in any of the following settings? *(Mark all that apply.)*

○ Pool   ○ Waterfront (Lake)
○ Beach (Ocean)   ○ Waterpark

21 Which of the following was a reason that you selected this course rather than a course at another time or location? *(Mark all that apply.)*

○ Employer arranged for course.
○ Location was convenient.
○ Needed course as soon as possible.
○ Day of the week was convenient.
○ Time of day was convenient.
○ Price was more reasonable than other choices.
○ Sponsoring agency has a good reputation.
○ Someone recommended this course.
○ Did not know of any other courses.
○ Other ▶ What? _____

22 Do you have any suggestions for improving this course?

_____
_____

23 Are you of Hispanic origin or background?

○ Yes   ○ No

24 Do you consider yourself:
○ White   ○ Asian
○ Black   ○ Other ▶ What?
_____

25 Do you regularly speak any language other than English with your family?

○ Yes   ○ No

26

Age		
⓪①②③④⑤⑥⑦⑧⑨		
⓪①②③④⑤⑥⑦⑧⑨		

27 Gender:

○ Male   ○ Female

28 What is the highest grade that you have completed?

○ Eighth grade or less
○ Some high school
○ Completed high school
○ Some college courses
○ Completed college
○ Graduate school

Chapter Code				Instructor Code			
⓪	⓪	⓪	⓪	⓪	⓪	⓪	⓪
①	①	①	①	①	①	①	①
②	②	②	②	②	②	②	②
③	③	③	③	③	③	③	③
④	④	④	④	④	④	④	④
⑤	⑤	⑤	⑤	⑤	⑤	⑤	⑤
⑥	⑥	⑥	⑥	⑥	⑥	⑥	⑥
⑦	⑦	⑦	⑦	⑦	⑦	⑦	⑦
⑧	⑧	⑧	⑧	⑧	⑧	⑧	⑧
⑨	⑨	⑨	⑨	⑨	⑨	⑨	⑨

Thank you for your help.